Spirit, Symbols, and Change among the Aymara

Spirit, Symbols, and Change among the Aymara

A Blind Shaman's Guide to a Maryknoll Missionary in Peru

INOCENTE SALAZAR

RESOURCE *Publications* · Eugene, Oregon

SPIRIT, SYMBOLS, AND CHANGE AMONG THE AYMARA
A Blind Shaman's Guide to a Maryknoll Missionary in Peru

Photograph credits: All photographs (03 – 19) in this book were taken by the author and are his property. Figures 01 and 02 are from different sources

Title page image: The "Gate of the Sun, Huirajocha at Tiwanaku (Spanish: Tiawana-ko). The eastern side of the "Gate of the Sun, Viracocha, at the ruins of Tiwanaku. The tears rolling down from the eyes depict a compassionate god.

Resource Publications
An Imprint of Wipf and Stock Publishers
199 W. 8th Ave., Suite 3
Eugene, OR 97401

www.wipfandstock.com

PAPERBACK ISBN: 978-1-7252-9381-6
HARDCOVER ISBN: 978-1-7252-9380-9
EBOOK ISBN: 978-1-7252-9382-3

03/22/21

This book is dedicated to my wife
Trinidad Cutipa
And the Aymara people she represents

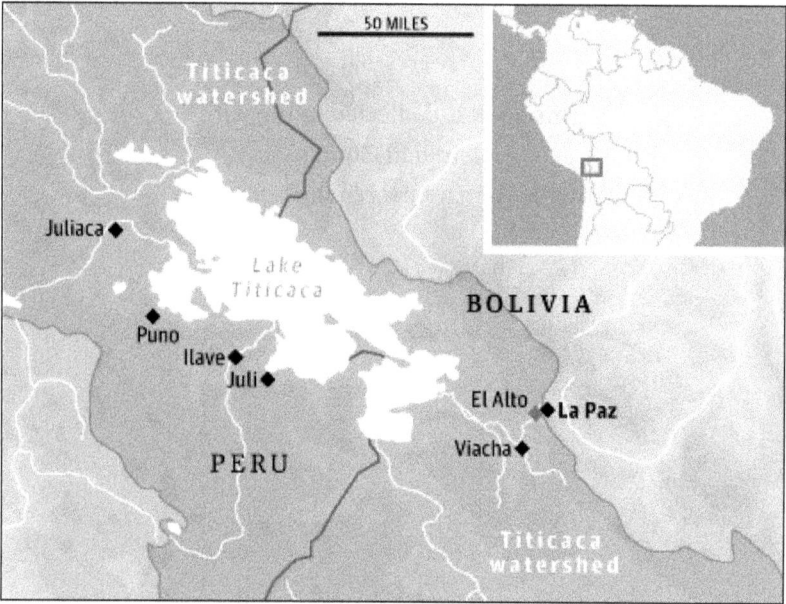

Figure 02.gif. Map localizing Ilave, the place of this study

Contents

Introduction

"No man ever steps in the same river twice,
For it's not the same river and he's not the same man."

—Heraclitus

My life has always been one of evoking and promoting change. This struck me one day when the members of the job training program where I worked visited a local company in Phoenix, Arizona, with the goal of placing some of our clients in that company. The personnel manager, Carla, a former student of mine, saw me and called me into her office; she related to me how she had changed so much from having taken my evening classes at Western International University. From three of my classes, she had learned a fresh approach in dealing with her staff, her employees and her bosses. The approach was very basic, take people as they are with their beliefs and lifestyles without any judgment on their value or usefulness. This kind of acceptance creates a new outlook on life for both students as well as the people with whom we work.

I was flattered to receive such a compliment; it made me keenly aware that I had always tried to bring about change for the betterment of others, especially forgotten and marginalized people. Carla's experience, as that of other students, was particularly impressive because, without my imposing something new, I had been able to engender some innovations. This incident made me look back to the 1970's at a period in my life in which this effort at change was my principal occupation; while transformation is natural and inevitable, I could direct it to specific goals. This book recounts this odyssey as a missionary to the Aymara of southern Peru, with

Marcelino Aduviri, a blind healer-shaman as my guide. I also illustrate the steps toward religious and social change.

The Aymara are an indigenous ethnic group who live around Lake Titicaca and on to La Paz, Bolivia. In the 1960's, they numbered about one and a half million in the Altiplano, the high plains region at an altitude of over 12,500 feet above sea level. The surface of Lake Titicaca is actually about 12,545 feet above sea level.[1] It did not take long for me to appreciate the Aymara.

I grew to love the Aymara described so differently in various anthropological studies. They exhibited so many everyday characteristics or quirks that made them loveable. For example, when the men took their hats off, their hair stood straight up like standing bundles of barley sheaves. They dressed in black homespun pants and white woolen shirts, along with a black homemade coat. When they offered to shake hands, they did not present their sweaty hands but offered their wrists to shake. Many times, their smiles would be green from chewing coca leaves to stave off hunger pangs or fatigue. The women wore derby hats, which they had adopted from English railroad workers in the late 1800's. They wore the bell-shaped skirt called *pollera* in Spanish. They wrapped their babies so tightly; they claimed this wrap kept their children's backs straight; and when they carried their babies on their backs, they trusted the simple knot on their *llijjllas* to keep the babies safe and secure. They have the habit of wiping their kids' runny noses with the inside hem of their skirts. It seemed they cleaned everything this way. They shared food generously with beggars at the market or on the street.

The young men gathered as if in a team ready to take on any challenger. They were a strong but shy lot. The young women were particularly modest and shy. They hid their smiles and laughter with shawl-covered hands; or they simply pulled their shawls up to hide their faces, like a turtle hides its head in its shell. The children were not shy at all. Whenever I arrived at a village, they would come up to me, hug my leg and say *m'tch'aya*, to ask for candy. M'tch'aya, is an onomatopoetic word depicting the sound of sucking on candy.

Old men and women would sit quietly and spin wool as they made conversation with me. I do not know if they understood me but they seemed to enjoy my company; I certainly enjoyed visiting with them.

Men and women used *t'amata*, fermented urine, to wash their hair, but I never smelled it. To me, all the people here smelled like new potatoes — except when they got wet in the rain. Then, they smelled like wet sheep because of their homespun woolens. In the villages, we would sit together

1. Tschopik, *The Aymara*, p.153.

in a smoke-filled kitchen; they claimed the smoke warmed them. Many times, I had to run outside for air; the heavy smoke choked me and made me cough and gasp. My eyes watered and everyone around me laughed, but still, we were at home with each other. All the time that we visited and enjoyed each other's company, I was always puzzled about how they survived so well by following the traditional ways that go back long before the Spanish conquest and even before the existence of the Inca empire. Although the Aymara have had over five centuries of foreign exposure, their traditional ways and their language have not changed. When I sought to resolve this puzzle of tradition, these very same people introduced me to a way of life so spiritual that it changed my life and the work of fellow missionaries as well as that of the Aymara.

This book is a fundamental look at the Aymara, their culture and the events that transformed whole villages as well as our mission practice. The first chapter is about my formative years of mission work, beginning with my arrival at the parish of San Miguel in Ilave, Peru, in October 1964. At this church, I had the pastoral duties of a Catholic priest, whose work was to transform a people to a life shaped by Catholic teachings and a lifestyle based on that Christian faith.

Chapter two links the Catholic practices of the Aymara to our ministry. There were, however, many anomalies; for example, people believed the cross without the crucified Christ is a person. This belief, among others, made it difficult to see the Aymara as Catholics.

Chapter three begins with my studying Clinical Pastoral Education (CPE) in the summer of 1970, which created for me a wholly different approach to ministry in which I learned to put peoples' spiritual needs before any preaching or moralizing. Ironically, it occurred to me to investigate why the Aymara in my charge adhered so tightly to their centuries' old life style and language. In the process, I became deeply involved in the native religiosity of the Aymara under the guidance of Marcelino Aduviri. The people who gave us potatoes now give us a new spirituality, which I discovered by attending their all-night ceremonies. I photographed and recorded these rituals, as well as conversations, all of which allowed me to study the meaning behind these unique religious sentiments, which do not relate to Catholic practice.

Chapter four begins with my presenting a new and profound view of the Aymara to fellow Maryknoll missionaries. Sharing these insights triggered a series of changes in our mission methodology from language learning to experimental liturgical practices.

Chapter five illustrates how we organized reflection-action groups by following the directives from liberation theology. These groups helped the

Aymara break away from the limitations that local prejudices had placed on them; these biases barred them from any possibility of becoming part of mainstream society.

Chapter six guides the reader to understand and develop symbolic language as the key element to consciously become part of the Aymara, or any other culture. Culture reveals itself through symbols, which, among others, include practices like courting customs, a child's first haircut, and naming the spirits that help or harm people. It is imperative for outsiders to develop a sensitivity to the symbols people use in everyday life and to know how to interpret them with the inevitable challenge to create new symbols. These chapters come from actual observation and participation with the Aymara in their religious rituals. In later research, I was able to corroborate and substantiate my conclusions as noted in the footnotes.

The seventh chapter reviews the major areas of change that I observed in the Aymara people, in the Maryknoll missionary colleagues and especially in me. The change I describe is one of establishing equality, a concept from Isaiah in which opposite forces in nature and in war come together in peaceful harmony. The wolf shall be the guest of the lamb, the baby shall play by the cobra's den and swords are forged into ploughshares; these images form the vision of equality in which justice reigns.[2] Consciously or unconsciously, I wanted to achieve that kind of transformation by teaching others how to make this change. Once denied a place in mainstream society, people would learn and exercise the freedom and the strength to stand up for themselves. These goals defined mission for me.

The concluding chapter is an overview of where I am now as I still exercise the transformation process I had experienced while working among the Aymara. This was true in teaching and in job placement counseling, as well as in being a volunteer at a St. Vincent de Paul food pantry, where we assist people of diverse backgrounds, including African-Americans and Mexican-Americans. These changes are not something we bring to a people as new and innovative; but rather, what the people themselves decide to change is what will remain true and permanent. For example, people living in poverty can discover and verbalize their condition as the first step out of poverty. They can break the mentality that forces them to be poor and to live within those limits; there is a way out. We are part of that change as our role is to be with them in their struggle and provide whatever makes that path out of poverty a firm path. The change comes from recognizing their values, their spirituality and the cultural practices corresponding to their needs. When we know and understand people, change follows.

2. Isaiah 11, 6–9; 42, 1–4.

Marcelino and author Salazar, on the left.

Acknowledgments

MY THANKS GO FIRST to the late Rev. Robert Cholke who asked me to gather data on natural sacrament with the goal of developing a new theology of sacrament. My research, however, began with the apparent non-change of the Aymara. That study led me to their religious practices and to their spiritual world. As I tried to give this study direction and application, Cholke provided expert advice and encouragement. His untimely death in April of 2007 left me to work on my own.

Although it is impossible to enumerate all the people who assisted me in Peru, there are several who deserve special thanks. Maria Tapia, who sold ritual elements in the Ilave market, understood my desire to understand the Aymara's tenacity in keeping to their old ways. She introduced me to Marcelino Aduviri, a local diviner and healer, who became my guide into the spiritual world of the Aymara. Marcelino took me into his company more as an apprentice rather than as a curious person. Another outstanding individual was Domingo Mamani, who accompanied me to these all-night rituals as interpreter and teacher. Later, Hipòlito Machaca and Trinidad Cutipa became strong leaders in our action-reflection groups. I cannot thank them enough for their contributions in facilitating discussions and activities as they accompanied me to this new world.

The many Aymara families that received us into their homes to observe, record and photograph also deserve my appreciation and thanks for their trust in us. I am grateful to our catechists, especially Pedro Copaja, who provided feedback on our groups; they filled me in on many details of daily life and related many of the folktales of the Aymara.

In contrast to the priests in the parish, the Sisters who worked within the Maryknoll missions were immensely supportive, especially Sister Jewell Rose Lorio; she asked a lot of questions for clarifying concepts of Aymara daily life and beliefs. She was able to utilize this newly found information in her classes at the local girls' school. Her knowledge of Aymara daily life cemented her relationship with her students. After she left Peru, she continued teaching at her Order's girls' high school in New Orleans and introduced the Aymara spiritual experience into her curriculum. I thank her for her questions, suggestions and her moving me to make my work public.

Within Maryknoll, Father Marty Murphy, my regional superior, interviewed me several times about my study of these rites. He recognized that this study contributed to developing a realistic approach to our mission in the Juli Prelature; eventually, his reports convinced Maryknoll to make a documentary film on my work.

When it came to writing about this experience, I just could not put this material together after several drafts. I am grateful to the various friends and colleagues, especially classmate Wally Inglis, who took time to read my scattered thoughts. Bill Hibbets and his wife, Kathleen, dedicated a great deal of time editing and clarifying my material. With their suggestions and my review of my field notes, I was able to give my writing some direction.

A special thanks goes to Joe Flocco, a retired free-lance photographer from New York; he prepared all my photographs into a publishing format. My granddaughter, Esperanza Salazar-Sampson, also deserves thanks for helping with the finishing touches on the pictures. I could not have gotten past this stage without their help.

The final help came for Dr. Mary Karasch, professor emerita from Oakland University. I am so grateful to her because she helped organize and give literary life to my writing. She provided editing and proof-reading while asking question about unclear or misplaced thoughts. She has been a godsend for my finishing this book.

Finally, a huge thank you to my wife, Trinidad; she is Aymara and helped with the vocabulary that came up in my field notes. I am even more grateful for her patience in putting up with my disappearing for hours at a time as I worked on this manuscript.

1

A Missionary to the Aymara

The Formative Years

*Take the first step in faith. You don't have to see the whole staircase,
just take the first step.*

—Martin Luther King, Jr.

WHEN I ARRIVED IN Peru on Oct. 5, 1964, my lifelong dream of being a missionary was at last a reality; it was my first mission assignment and I was happy. This was a long time coming since I had entered the seminary at age fourteen; thirteen years later I was ordained a priest at age 27 and elated that I was finally in Peru. But how did I ever become a missionary? It began when I was in St. Boniface grammar school in Anaheim, California, and I received a magazine called *Maryknoll,* a gift subscription from Marie Ott, an elderly lady from the parish. Once I became interested in missionary work and told people about it, the priest from the parish, Father Thomas Cosgrove, followed up and even took me on sick calls. He talked to me frequently about the priesthood and introduced me to every recruiting priest that came to speak at our parish, but Maryknoll was the only mission group that I wanted to join.

I began my studies at the high school seminary in Mountain View, California, where we lived in the Maryknoll seminary. The building was on the top of a hill, built in Chinese style with the edges of the roof curved outward; the neighbors called it Tibet on the hill. Maryknoll adopted this style since its first missions had been in China and other parts of Asia. We attended classes at St. Joseph's College, the diocesan seminary, run by the Sulpician Fathers whose whole mission was to educate men for the priesthood. Throughout my studies, I pictured myself walking on rainy paths through hot and humid rice paddies, meeting with people in search of salvation; I visualized attending to human needs, such as providing food, clothing, and education. My dream had no limits, but the reality would be quite different once I went to the highlands of Peru.

Journey to Peru

The thrill of finally making it to my mission so overwhelmed me that I remember many details of the voyage and arrival in Peru even to this day. Twelve of us new missionaries had traveled together to Peru. We had left New York ten days before and traveled by cargo ship. Fred Smith, Bob Hoffman, Brother Aquinas, Brother Barnabas, and I were assigned to Peru. Bob Matthews, Ernie Lukachek, Frank Perulli, and Tom Adams were going to Chile after attending the Maryknoll Language School in Cochabamba, Bolivia. Frank Gerace, Dick Ramsey, and Bill Lafferty were off to Bolivia. Our first stop was Panama, where it had taken a full day to cross the Panama Canal.

From Panama, we made a stop in Colombia to unload and load cargo. Some men came on board and moved quickly among us offering us fistfuls of dollars for cigarettes, jeans, whiskey and other goods to sell on the black market. We told them we had nothing to sell, so they moved about the vessel to close their deals. At dusk, when the ship was pulling away from the dock, we saw some deck hands throwing boxes overboard, as canoes from the shore hurried to pick up their contraband.

When we reached Guayaquil, Ecuador, we were allowed to go ashore; it was late, almost evening, when we got a cab to go into town and wandered about marveling at how different this city was. As we walked about, there was a wave of shouting students running through the streets with the police and military after them. We panicked and tried going into one or another store, but storekeepers were frantically shutting their sliding steel doors. We tried to get out of the way or hide, but some soldiers confronted us and pointed rifles in our faces; an officer came up right away and pulled his sword out, and held it about waist high to halt the soldiers. He told them, "These men are foreigners. We'll escort them away from here."

He and a few soldiers took us to a street where there were no demonstrators; we could not get a cab fast enough to head back to our ship. We were stunned and we did not even know what to say about this experience;

however, Frank Gerace put the incident into perspective. This was one of many student protests against the government—a frequent occurrence in any Latin American country and would be something to contend with in mission.

We continued on to Trujillo in northern Peru. It was full daylight and we took a cab into town. The cab driver invited us to drink some *chicha*, a corn beer native to Peru, and drove us around the main plaza where an APRA rebellion had taken place. APRA is a political party, popular among young voters and very anti-military. In the mid 1930's, many had died in a confrontation between students of the APRA party and the Peruvian army.

We finally arrived in Callao, the principle port of Peru, where we were to disembark with all our belongings. As we were docking, there were four Maryknollers waiting for us at the dock. When they saw me, they laughed loudly and yelled to me," You're going to Ilave," and they broke out laughing again as if it were a big joke to them.

We went directly from the port to the Maryknoll Center house, excited to be so close to our new homes. After an incredibly good lunch, we had a tour of the parishes under the care of Maryknoll priests and brothers. Later, as my classmates and I went for a tour of Lima, the capital of Peru, everything seemed amazingly familiar to me as if I were in East Los Angeles. We were on Avenida Arequipa, when, suddenly, down the corner from where we were standing, there was a collision and one car overturned. We wanted to run and help but a crowd gathered quickly and up righted the tipped car. The first car that knocked the second one over had taken off; and as soon as the second car was upright, the driver took off after the one who had hit him. At the very moment of the accident, I said, "I feel like I haven't left home." Somehow (except for the accident), this scene reminded me of a Los Angeles street. My companions were visibly tense, but I thought it was from witnessing an accident. Later at supper, one of them said, "Back there when you said you felt like you had never left home, I was ready to punch you in the mouth." He explained that they were so tense from being in a new country without knowledge of the language; they felt lost, while I felt at home.

I spent three weeks in Lima while I waited for my visa to be processed. In the meantime, Fr. John Lawler, pastor of Santa Rosa de Lima parish, had me stay at his parish, and, since I already spoke Spanish, assigned me some Masses and other tasks. I became involved quickly in parish work, conducting meetings with church groups, visiting the sick, performing funeral services and conducting an informal census or simply visiting people in the parish to have them be aware of the services we provided. It looked like I was going to be absorbed into Santa Rosa parish; somehow, ministry at Santa Rosa was like working in an urban parish in the United States, and did not fit my notion of mission. In the seminary, I had developed concepts of mission from three books by Rowland Allen, who looked at St. Paul's method of establishing churches with the local converts in charge of those new churches; but Santa Rosa was an American parish in a foreign country. My assignment could have easily been changed so that I would not make it to my destination of Ilave, the butt of one big joke among Maryknollers.

Then one day, a young man from the parish high school invited me to go see a movie titled "Kukuli", a film recorded in Quechua and narrated in Spanish. I did not know Quechua or the region of Cuzco where the film had been made. What I saw were the Quechua going about their everyday chores amid the expansive landscape with the wind tossing the grassy tufts about like a dance to nature. I recalled my childhood days when we lived on the ranch outside of Rocksprings, Texas, where I was born. Dad was a ranch hand and he used to take me with him when he and my grandfather were mending fences; while they worked, I played in the grassy fields and the wind moved the grass about as in this movie. I walked out of that movie with no other thought than to get to Ilave and work with the native population there, and when I got to the parish, I called the Center House to inquire about my residency papers. The next day, the secretary, Carlos, picked me up to go to the Ministry of Interior, where I was photographed, and went from desk to desk until I obtained my visa. At each desk, the official had a little carousal of rubber stamps; as he reviewed my papers, he twirled that rack until he found the right stamp for my papers and sent me off to another desk for a similar procedure.

Carlos obtained a plane ticket to Arequipa, where I would spend the night at the Cerro Colorado parish, the center house for the Maryknoll missionaries in that part of the country. From there I was to travel by train to Puno. The advice I got from the priests in Arequipa was that I should not eat too much because of the altitude; I would be living at 12,500 feet above sea level. Furthermore, I was not to carry heavy stuff, like my luggage.

The train trip to Arequipa was eight hours long and slow and I got very hungry during that trip. A waiter came through the car offering meals from the diner car; I ordered a meal, while somewhat worried about eating too much. I quickly finished the tepid meal and I was still hungry. The train stopped at every town on the way to Puno. It seemed to me that these were just villages as the towns appeared to be very small. Vendors ran up to the train at every stop and I bought some snacks, and I was still hungry; by now, I was not too careful about limiting my eating. Finally, we began seeing larger towns, such as Juliaca, which was a bustling center and a few miles from Puno, where I would go to San Juan parish for the night before continuing on to Ilave. When I got off the train, I felt fine; I had no upset stomach or aches from eating so much. The priest who came for me took my bag from my hand although I had carried it about three train car lengths before we met. I felt no strain or dizziness. "You have to be careful carrying heavy things in the altitude," he told me. He drove me to San Juan parish where the priests received me warmly. The parish residence was located on a top floor over the nave of the church.

Ilave

The next day, Pat Riley, associate pastor at San Miguel parish in Ilave, came for me, and we drove to Ilave over a corrugated road, the main highway between Peru and Bolivia. The drive over this bouncy road created so much noise in the jeep that we had to talk very loudly to hear each other. Pat told me, "Get used to bouncing on these roads. They're all like this after the rains." He pointed out the Maryknoll staffed churches in each town we passed. "Ilave is the biggest parish in this region," he said.

When we reached San Miguel, Pat introduced me to Tom Higgins, my new pastor, who greeted me with: "Welcome, now you have to hurry to do a mission. Pat will take you to the *Estancia.*" Estancia, a farm in Spanish, is what the early Spaniards called the Indian villages; the traditional name was *ayllu.* The mission in this case was a pastoral visit to a village consisting of hearing confessions, celebrating Masses and baptizing some infants. Tom's quick greeting and his orders to go out to a village gave me the impression that Tom was totally serious; an all-work-and-no-play kind of guy. He was about six feet tall, wore glasses, and he seemed to wear his cassock most of the time. His face was somewhat square and ruddy; when I met him, he was busy with some paperwork while smoking his pipe.

The first Mass I celebrated at my first mission was on October 28, 1964, at an Aymara estancia. At Mass, I gave a brief homily in Spanish, but the congregation was unresponsive. I thought there would be at least a glimmer of understanding and some kind of rapport. I soon realized that the people did not speak or understand Spanish, only Aymara. This was the first of many shocking frustrations. I reflected on the prayer of St. Francis of Assisi who said, "It is better to understand than be understood." After I spoke, the local catechist gave a brief translation of my sermon.

Afterwards, Tom gave me a tour of the parish complex. After my first impression of Tom, he now appeared friendly and genuinely interested that I learn quickly the parish routine and the people working there. Tom introduced me to the office staff, Maria and Hipólito. Maria had a dark complexion with very black hair and lapdog eyes. Hipolito was also bronzed-skinned with long eyelashes and no facial hair, a true Aymara. Both appeared to be very shy.

Across town were the convent and a boarding school formally run by Columbian nuns who were now gone. Tom was negotiating a contract with some American nuns to work in his school. Occupying the school center were two Papal volunteers, and their housekeeper, Trinidad Cutipa. The parish staff all looked the same in those first few days, but Trinidad stood out with a wonderfully captivating personality; she was the first Aymara woman I had met. She was well known to the priests in Ilave since she had worked with the Maryknoll missionaries since their arrival in 1954.

Catechists

A few days later I met the catechists. The greater part of our work was done through catechists, since most of the missionaries did not speak Aymara. The catechists were chosen from various communities or estancias to instruct and guide their people in Christian doctrine and a Christian way of life, especially in receiving the sacraments; they met regularly with the pastor and other priests for instruction on what to do for one week ahead. One catechist, Marcelino Coaquira, was particularly adept at giving instruction for baptism each Sunday before Mass. For almost all the parishioners, this was really the only time to connect instruction about the sacrament of baptism with the actual baptizing of the babies. Parents and godparents sat through an hour's talk in Aymara on the meaning of baptism and the responsibility for both parent and sponsor.

Although catechists were simple farmers, they exhibited certain leadership qualities that got them chosen as catechists. They took their job seriously since they were leaders and they spoke for the priest. Fr. Tom Verhoeven had started a catechetical school at the parish in the town of Azangaro and all the other parishes quickly followed suit in training their catechists along the line of Fr. Verhoeven's school. In spite of this training, the catechists knew enough in Spanish so that they could communicate with and understand the priests, but with many limitations; the catechists also needed an interpreter. Perhaps, with further instruction, the catechists were the ones to establish and maintain the Church among the Aymara. When St. Paul established the church, he quickly put it in the hands of the new converts.

> . . .the example of the Apostle to the Gentiles must be of the first importance to us. . . In a very few years, he built the Church on so firm a basis that it could live and grow in faith and in practice,

that it could work out its own problems and overcome all dangers and hindrances both from within and without."[1]

My first few years consisted of my carrying out my duties as a priest with all the formality of my office. Tom described the parish as having some 100,000 members, with a meager few inhabitants who were not baptized Catholics, but who belonged to the Northern Irish Baptist church; others belonged to an Adventist church-congregation. I was so pleased to have so many Catholics under our care. Each Sunday there were anywhere from forty to seventy infant baptisms. This high number of baptisms, as it turned out, was the basis for the joke on me when I arrived in Peru; no other parish in this region was so busy. This rate of baptisms gave us an indication of the need for our instructing and guiding people in the Catholic faith.

However, I learned early that people often baptized their children more out of fear than faith. They believed that their spirits would send them hail storms if they allowed a child to die without baptism. This belief and the high rate of infant mortality kept our baptismal numbers very high. With the help of the catechists, we tried to correct existing misconceptions about baptism and other religious practices. The catechists, however, were more like interpreters rather than experienced ministers of the church.

Such a belief motivated us to visit the villages on a regular basis to undo misconceptions about God, the Church, and the sacraments. Given the large numbers in this parish, it was normal to spend a lot of time celebrating Mass, baptizing, visiting villages and anointing the sick. The catechists prepared the people with having them memorize twenty-one questions and answers. Once they learned this material, the priest came out to celebrate a Mass, hear confessions and anoint the sick. People also asked for numerous blessings, which were not exactly evangelizing or even proselytizing. While all of us missionaries shared the same goal of establishing the Church, we were a long way from launching a Church that could function on its own.

On Sundays, I presided at a sub-parish church in the village of Cusullaca where the Maryknoll Fathers had built a small cinderblock chapel. Working at this sub-parish gave me positive impressions of the Aymara whom I loved because they were so different from what an anthropologist, Harry Tschopik, had described in his book, *The Aymara of Chucuito, Peru*, a study he had conducted from 1940 to 1942. Tschopik also quotes other anthropologists' descriptions of the Aymara as "submissive, sad, uncommunicative, distrustful" or as "capable of intense hatred and horrible cruelties" along with many other negative descriptions.[2] I started reading Tschopik

---

1. Allen, *Missionary Methods*, 7.
2. Tschopik, *The Aymara*, 172–174.

shortly after I got to Ilave but stopped because he described the Aymara in such a negative light. This study emphasized the cheerless side of the Aymara. He includes several anthropologists' focus on the "truculent, hostile, unsmiling, humble, melancholy, submissive, notoriously sullen, somber, and morose" aspects of the Aymara personality.

Since Tschopik did not speak Aymara, much of his information had to be translated by the non-Aymara townspeople informants, who are called *mistis,* perhaps a shortened form of mestizo, and who exercise a strict hierarchical social structure in which the "Indian" is out of the social mainstream. Mistis exhibit a particular kind of prejudice toward the Aymara and exact total compliance to their assumed aristocracy base on a partial Spanish ancestry rather than race. For example, Tschopik observed that the Aymara greeted the misti by dropping to one knee and tipping his or her hat, bow, and greet the misti in a whiny voice.[3] I heard those same high-pitched greetings as: "*Buenos días, Huirajocha,*" "*Buenos días, Ñita,*" :Good day Sir, good day, Miss. From what people told me, ñitas referred to young women of the Spanish royal household. These misti families referred to themselves as being of blue blood or of Spanish bloodlines. Blue referred to the very white skin that made the veins appear very blue. This racial distinction kept the Aymara from ever claiming anything or any justice.

One can understand how the Aymara might be pessimists. They live at the timberline; Ilave is at 14,000 feet above sea level. They go against the odds and farm the lands when the only water supply is the rain that may or may not come. At that height, they have to contend with frosts, hail, and windstorms. Even their own resources are limited as the cost of seed and fertilizers keeps going up. They invest a lot of work in what is simply putting food on the table; this is subsistence farming.

Introduction to the Aymara Belief System

From my having to celebrate Mass at the outlying villages, as well as in the parish church, I encountered a number of practices that appeared odd to me as they did not correspond to Catholic practices I knew so well. What really made our pastoral tasks so time consuming was the insistence of the people for what I thought were odd requests. For example, there were those who often came to Mass with cans of kerosene or bundles of flowers to be blessed; they claimed these blessed items would ward off hail storms as long as a priest blessed them; there was a magical effect from these blessings. If a priest refused to give the blessing, these same people rushed to

3. Tschopik, *The Aymara,* 159.

the front of the congregation to catch the end of Mass blessing. This was one of the practices that gave the priest an immensely important role in the Aymara's life.

The priests themselves were not exempt from other magical notions. The people often described the priest as a *liq'ichiri,* a collector of human fat for making holy oils for church use. People describe the *liq'ichiri,* (also known as *kharisiri)* as a priest, usually a Franciscan friar, who wanders about at night to hypnotize his victims, makes them sleep, then, cuts a small incision just to the right of the abdomen to extract the fat from around the liver. On one occasion, Pedro Mamani from Huancuni, not far from town, called for me because he was dying. When he saw me, he claimed to recognize me as the *liq'ichiri* who had cut him and now he was dying. I told him it must have been some other spirit because I was home the evening before, but he insisted on his story and even showed me his incision that looked like a scratch, something hardly fatal, but he died the following day.

Tom introduced me to some other local beliefs and customs. He began by giving me a small bundle that fitted in the palm of my hand. It contained a couple of talismans and wool in the shape of a nest and colored strings.

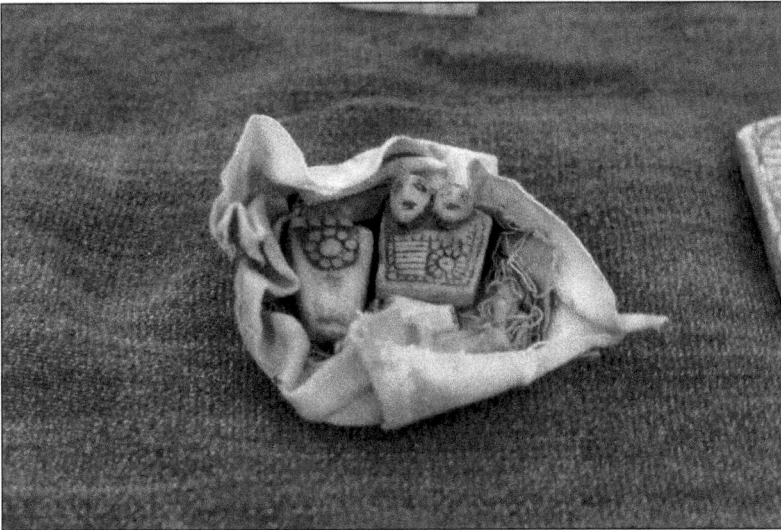

Talisman for a perfect marriage. Stone figure includes the couple, their lands and a wealth protection. The person using this talisman is serious about his marriage and its success.

Tom explained how a young man uses this particular packet to find and obtain the perfect wife, a procedure that involved consulting the local shaman for the necessary ceremony to draw this woman to marry this man. Once they decide to marry, the man brings his bride to spend a month with the prospective mother–in-law to test this woman's ability to be a good wife. If she passes the test, the couple is married.

Tom chuckled at this last detail that if the young woman becomes pregnant during the testing period and fails, the young man's family will raise the child of their temporary union. This frees a woman to have another chance to pass the mother–in-law test and to marry. I was impressed with Tom's detailed knowledge of local customs. This story was very interesting but what really caught my attention was Tom's telling me how people often put talismans or other ritual objects under the saints' statues in the church; the idea that the Indians used the statues in church for their own rituals was repulsive to me. In later research, I traced that this practice has a long history and was recorded in 1621 by Father Pablo Joseph Arriaga, a Jesuit missionary, in his book, *The Extirpation of Idolatry in Peru*.[4] Arriaga seemed to have defined mission as making all inhabitants totally Catholic, Spanish Catholics, by destroying their religion. By this time, I was sure the people here were idolatrous and not true Christians.

Once I became aware of the nature of these objects and of the requests made of the priests, I was convinced that the people were idolatrous and decided to launch my own program to combat these practices. I turned to Ezekiel 14, 1—5, in which the prophet condemned the people and prophets who kept the memory of their idols. From what Tom had told me, I figured that I could not be wrong to tell people that they were practicing the wrong religion. I preached what I thought were powerful sermons, but I had no idea whether the catechists' translations reached the people or that I even made a dent in the people's thinking and practice.

On one occasion, I deliberately kicked over candles lit before a statue of San Isidro, the patron saint of oxen, farm fields and rain. My objective was to divert their attention to the Mass and not to a statue of the saint driving a yoke of oxen. Numerous people came to church, not to attend Mass, but to sit or kneel and watch how their candles burned. It did not take long for me to realize how wrong I was in the way I acted. San Isidro was more important to them than any Mass since the people believed that the saint's plowing would produce the rain needed for good and plentiful crops. When I told Tom what I did, he just shook his head and said nothing; I had fallen into a trap of treating them the way many others treated Indians, as ignorant and superstitious.

4. Arriaga, *The Extirpation*, 58.

As the people continued to exhibit what I saw as strange forms of religion, I attained a strong motive for learning the local language if I was going to be effective in my mission. Our work appeared to be quite mechanical with the prevailing requests for blessings without a Catholic meaning to them; I was beginning to define a little more clearly the concept of mission.

2

Saints and Catholic Rituals of the Aymara

"The gospel always comes to people in cultural robes. There is no such thing as a 'pure' gospel, isolated from culture"[1]

CONNECTING THE AYMARA TO Catholicism seemed logical when celebrating Mass for the patron saint of a village; however, that link became somewhat blurry when the catechists described how that saint was seen and why he/she was venerated with a Mass. My duty was to provide Mass in honor of these saints at the request of these baptized Christians. However, just as baptism had its overtone of placating the spirits, the Mass likewise took on similar magical overtones. Having the saints hear the Mass fulfilled the needs of the people.

1. Bosch. *Transforming*, p.297.

Village saints at church "to hear Mass" by which the spirits of these images also conform to the official religion as an added strength to their power.

The Saint-Catholicism began with first Spanish missionaries as they conducted a policy of destroying ancient rituals and shrines dedicated to local spirits; they filled the churches with statues of saints to serve as reminders and examples of a good Christian life. However, the Aymara saw in the saints the faces of the spirits from their world since they considered them to be small like the statues; the statues corresponded to their practices and beliefs and to the role the saints and spirits play in people's lives.

May 3 was the feast of the Holy Cross or Santa Cruz. The cross is depicted with a face but not a crucified body of Jesus as traditionally depicted in Catholic churches. People consider Santa Cruz, the cross itself, to be a saint, and is depicted with a face at the crossbeams, making it a person. This cross is different from the traditional crucified Christ, which is not found in Aymara chapels.

The spirit called Santa Cruz (Holy Cross) is not a Christian cross but a spirit named Santa Cruz. It has a face at the cross beams to identify it as a person or spirit. Village chapels have this cross; rarely is the crucified Christ found

San Isidro Labrador, whose day is May 14, became the patron saint of rain and good crops; St. Anthony, June 13, is the patron of pigs; St. Bartholomew, August 24, the patron of lawyers and legal suits; and St John the Baptist, June 24, the patron of sheep and alpacas. St. John's day corresponds to the summer solstice of the southern hemisphere. It is like a new year and the people participate in fortune telling to perceive what the coming year would bring both for themselves and for their animals.

Trinity Sunday was the feast of cattle and *Corpus Christi*, the feast of the people. The dates of these two feasts depended on the date of Easter and changed from year to year. There were many other saints who corresponded to some cycle in one's life. We celebrated Mass for many of these saints without our knowing the exact religious sentiment behind each saint.

The major feasts of the Virgin Mary corresponded to the quarterly stages of farming, thereby equating the Virgin Mary to the earth goddess, *Pachamama*. The feast of Natividad or the birth of the Virgin Mary on September 8, corresponds to sowing a new crop; la Imaculada, the feast of the Immaculate Conception, on December 8, offers the first view of the potatoes; the faithful adorn the statue with potatoes on that day.

Statue of the "Imaculada" the Virgin Mary adorned with potatoes at their early stage. Their size and form foretell of a good crop. Mary is seen as Pachamama, Mother Earth.

February 2, Candelaria recalls Mary presenting the infant Jesus at the temple; this feast generally coincides with the time of Carnival; for the Aymara, people recall the birth of the potato.

Local people celebrate the birth of the potato and the beginning of farming at Carnival; they place bundles of potatoes in a place of prominence, sprinkle them with wine and confetti and dance as homage to them.

The feast of Our Lady of Mount Carmel on July 16 matches the season for freeze-drying and storing potatoes for the coming year.

Andean people freeze dry the potatoes shortly after the harvest when the frost sets in. They lay the potatoes on the ground where they freeze at night. The potatoes swell up with the morning sun. The people, then, squeeze the juice out of them with their bare feet. Wearing shoes for this procedure offends Mother Earth. They repeat this procedure over three days. Finally, the juice-free potatoes are left to dry in the sun, gathered and stored, sometimes for years. These are called *ch'uño*. Archeologists have discovered *ch'uño* in the coastal graves of mummified bodies, well preserved, ready to be soaked and cooked. This simple and natural way of preserving food reflects the genius of the Aymara in attending to their needs for long periods of time.

While these feasts of the Virgin Mary are not an exact calendar for the cycles of the potato, it helped the people to put a face on the Pachamama who gave them the good crops and healthy animals.

There are two saints who are especially feared, namely, Santiago or St James and his consort, Santa Bárbara, both of whom are patrons or controllers of lightning, a killer element in this region. St. James fell naturally into the role of keeper and hurler of lightning and death as drawn from

St. Mark's gospel in which he and his brother are described as the sons of thunder in Mark, 3, 17. In Luke 9, 54, James and John asked Jesus, "Do you want us to call down fire from heaven to consume them (Samaritan villagers)"? Although the Aymara may not have made these connections, the Spanish preachers must have taken advantage of both the gospel imagery and indigenous beliefs to give St. James such an awesome position of the hurler of death. Arriaga relates in his *Extirpation of Idolatry in Peru,* that the ancient name for lightning was *Illapa.* He is described as the *Viracocha* with the *illapa* in his hand.[2]

Santiago Matamoros is a Spanish saint depicted on horseback, piercing a fallen enemy with a spear, usually a Moor or a person of color.

Santiago in mullu form. Note that Santiago's victim is a white skin devil. Spanish depictions place a person of color as the target of Santiago's spear.

2. Arriaga, *Extirpation,* 23.

In Andean tradition, the spear represents his lightning bolt. As the god of lightning, he is most feared because he possesses power to destroy crops and life. After a lightning strike, the shaman usually looks for a bullet from Santiago; this "bullet" is usually a round musket ball.

The "bala de Santiago" is a musket ball found at the site of a lightning strike. These two are gifts from a local yatiri. At the sight of these, people remove their hats, pray and touch the "bala" to their foreheads.

This belief that Santiago sends bolts of lightning came with the Spanish from Galicia. A filmmaker friend wrote to me with this information: in Galicia, an arrowhead marked the place of the strike. A *pacco* gave me one of these bullets. When I showed it to villagers, they took off their hats in respect, kissed it and prayed to it. This was not simply a remnant or a symbol of Santiago but the saint himself.

When the parish clinic suffered a fire, some of the townspeople told me that as the flames shot upward, they saw Santiago riding away on his white horse. For them, Santiago no longer resided at the Santa Barbara church, located next to the parish clinic. An early chronicler, Huaman Poma, in his book *Letter to a King (Nueva Corònica y Buen Gobierno)*, gives a similar description:

. . .St James of Galicia, according to those who were present, made his appearance in the form of a clap of thunder followed by a shaft of light which illuminated the Inca fortress of Sacsahuaman above the city. The Indians were terrified at the idea that Illapa, the thunder and lightning, had descended from the sky. And many witnesses testified that St. James descended on a white horse with a plume on his head and jingling bells and trappings. The Saint was dressed in a white cape and carried a banner. He was armed with a shield and a naked sword, with which he caused great havoc and killed a multitude of Indians, breaking up the encirclement of the Christians and forcing Manco Inca into flight.[3]

When the first Spaniards were involved in skirmishes with the Indians, they yelled, "Santiago, Santiago" and fired their harquebuses or muskets, creating a flame and thunderous roar. As a result, *Illapa* and Santiago became synonymous. Santiago is the saint that Pizarro invoked as he attacked and captured Atahualpa, the Inca leader, and slaughtered most of the Inca's men on November 16, 1532.[4] The Inca and his men were caught unawares and unarmed and were viciously defeated and slaughtered. Knowing this history, I wondered, if behind the contemporary fear of Santiago, was the fear of the marauding outsider who could kill them without provocation.

In Aymara belief, the consort of Santiago is Santa Bárbara. This Catholic saint may have lived in the time of the early Church when the Romans were killing Christians for their beliefs. Barbara was the daughter of a Roman nobleman; she converted to Christianity while her father remained a pagan. When he arranged a marriage with a young nobleman, Barbara refused because the young suitor was not a Christian. Her father was furious with Barbara and locked her in a prison tower and eventually had her executed for disobeying him. The Aymara altered the traditional Hispanic story so that Barbara killed her father by hurling a sword-like bolt of lightning at him. I visited the cathedral of Ayacucho where Barbara is depicted as holding a long sword with the head of her father at the point of the sword. In religious goods stores, Barbara is depicted with the tower and the sword but not the father's head. A similar story is told in an article on the use of saint statues to instruct the people.[5]

The longevity of these beliefs and practices appeared to me as symbolic of the nearly five hundred years of Aymara resistance to the Catholic

3. Huaman Poma, *Letter*, p. 115.

4. Cieza, *The Discovery*, p.212; and note 8, p. 214.

5. Ortega, *Andean*, no.50

religion, to modern farming practices and to the social structures of the outsiders. For these four centuries, the Aymara continued to believe in and practice their own religion. Centered on traditional spirits, the statues of the saints in the churches helped preserve their ancient ancestral spirits. It became clear that this saint-related Catholicism was a different religious expression from what the Spanish missionaries had instituted; it supported the Aymara life-giving rituals with the use of, or reliance on the saints' statues. We had let the practice continue without limiting or reigning it in to a more authentically Catholic practice. I was not sure where to go with this scant knowledge of Aymara practices; they seemed well enough not to disturb or discontinue since they linked the Aymara to the Church. Even the role of the Catholic priest was somewhere within this pantheon-like world of spirits and saints. Adding to the mystery of the priest, very few missionaries spoke the language of the people, and that language gap interfered with communicating the essence of the Catholic faith.

Personnel Changes

In contrast, I learned so much from Tom Higgins, about the Aymara, the culture, and the language. I loved working with him because he had such a commanding knowledge of the people and of their customs, and he was so close to them. Most people did not realize how fluent Tom was in the language until one time, he overheard a conversation about a killing that had taken place in one of the villages. When he asked in Aymara where this incident happened, the group dropped the subject and spoke no more since Tom could understand them.

Working with Tom seemed like all-work-and-no-play. A day off for either of us came once every six or eight weeks. Our parish was very busy with missions to the villages, the special groups and, of course, the multitude of baptisms on weekends; no other parish had baptisms as numerous as ours. This did not include the weddings, funerals and visits to the sick. Besides the activity in the parish, the reason we had infrequent days off was that we, who worked on the Altiplano, were given a month long stay twice a year on the coast. The two vacations were to prevent whatever ailments might result from working at 12,000 to 14,000 feet above sea level.

Tom had a dry sense of humor and often told of his experiences with a touch of humor. He loved classical music, especially the couple of operas we had on LP records. When the Dominican Sisters arrived from New Orleans, Louisiana, to run the parish school, Tom opened up more. Sisters Bridget and Jane were the first to arrive. Sister Sebastian arrived a few weeks later.

We would have dinner together on special occasions, or even a rare but enjoyable picnic. Before he laughed with a subdued chuckle but now, he could laugh more heartily, especially when he was the butt of the joke.

The sisters were very personable in their dealings with the people both in town and in the villages. They worked very hard at the school and at a makeshift clinic we had in the parish. They invited Dr. Bob Ayerst, a physician friend of theirs, to come visit the Sisters' mission. He was even able to attend to a good number of ill people in the parish and even taught us how to administer first aid care and antibiotics and how to identify those who needed immediate medical care.

Three years after my arrival in Ilave, Tom was transferred to another parish. He left Peru shortly after his transfer, and began the process of asking Rome to release him from his vows so that he could marry. I owed him so much for teaching me to be a dedicated missionary and for teaching me about the people I was to serve. I felt his loss deeply even though two years earlier, a young priest had also left to marry.

I continued my work with the new pastor, Javier (Harvey), who introduced some innovative programs, such as creating a parish council made up of townspeople. They were to initiate and administer programs for the growth of the parish. Javier was a wonderful addition to the parish of San Miguel; he spent a lot of time praying both in church and in his room. I was highly impressed until he also left a year later to marry a nun with whom he had worked in the retreat program. His leaving shook my self-confidence, but not as much as with Tom's departure. With Javier, three priests had left with the intention of marrying. More power to them was my only thought. While Javier was pastor, the regional superior sent me to the Maryknoll Language School to study Aymara.

Language School: Aymara

Finally, after five years in Ilave, language school was a welcome assignment because I knew I needed the help of a professional instructor. Up to this point, my Aymara was dreadful. One woman once told me, "Your Aymara is terrible. You should marry a nice Aymara girl and learn Aymara well." I never expected that kind of criticism and that kind of advice from the people. The Aymara have a great sense of humor.

When I first arrived at the Altiplano, I did not have to learn Spanish, which was my first language. However, it did not take long for me to appreciate the need for learning Aymara. One time while visiting an old man who was dying, I stood by helplessly while the family surrounded the sick man and cried aloud. I wanted to console them but did not have the words. I had given my blessing and the Sacrament of the Sick, which is administered to anyone who is seriously ill.

Even though the sacrament and blessing to this dying man were sufficient, I also wanted to communicate my sympathies. I said a few words through the sacristan, my interpreter. He spoke at length in expressing my sympathies and his. Afterwards, he pointed out to me in an almost scolding way my need to know the local language. I felt the same need myself. Learning Aymara was not taken seriously by many of the missionaries, and, at the time, I was not aware of any program that was available for learning Aymara. Tom, who spoke Spanish, Aymara and Quechua extremely well, taught me the psychology of the people along with some basic Aymara.

Some priests argued that since mainstream society used Spanish, the natives needed to learn Spanish; and, if they spoke only Spanish, the Aymara would have to learn Spanish. The scant use of Aymara, however, was a problem to me. In contrast, Maryknoll Father Robert Kearns sought to teach Spanish to the monolingual villagers by means of Radio Schools. He founded a radio station named Onda Azul, and distributed single frequency radios to the villages. He transmitted classes for learning Spanish at various hours during the day. He also transmitted music, news and religious programs. His concept was original and innovative.

Using only Spanish in ministering to the people was not a problem for the Church. This conclusion is derived from the theological concept that sacraments work *ex opere operato,* that is, the sacraments give grace in spite of the language (or even moral) disposition of the minister. The trouble with this concept is that it gives sacraments a kind of magical power. The Church had used Latin as its official language for centuries and many loved this mysterious atmosphere of Latin. In 1967, the Second Vatican Council ordered the use of the local language in each church, and there were many who disapproved of the disappearance of the magic of Latin. The Andean people had their system of magic to begin with, and the sacrament, conducted by an official, was simply another kind of magic in their lives.

The priests that knew the language were few. Tom Higgins was one. Besides him, I knew of only three others, but Jim O'Brian and Tom were the only ones who used the language on a daily basis. The priests on the other side of the lake may have been fluent for all I know. All the missionaries had catechists who helped with instructing and translating; they were a tremendous help in communicating with the faithful; nevertheless, speaking the local language seemed to be a logical and natural goal for me and a very important part of mission. Without speaking Aymara, I could not imagine how the priests were able to discern and assess the spiritual needs of the people.

Tom started me off with simple phrases to use in confession and in visiting the sick. I never understood a confession in the beginning. I used some phrases to greet people before Mass. I always prefaced my attempt at Aymara with: "Don't laugh at me if I say things wrong." People immediately became grim. I think they were trying hard to control their wanting to laugh. Aymara was very hard to pronounce correctly.

The Ilave market was my school for Aymara. I learned the language, customs, and details on clothing, and the way in which people talk to each other. I practiced speaking by using recordings of ongoing conversations in the market. I transcribed those recordings phonetically as I had learned from an initial training in phonetics in the seminary.

I continued to learn Aymara and managed to put together some canned sermons. Although the structure of the language was relatively easy to understand and apply, pronunciation challenged me most. The language is made up of root words. Creating full sentences involved adding suffixes to the root word. A good example is a general word to take or to carry. The general word in Aymara meaning to carry is *apaña*.

I carry	aptwa	apa + t + wa
I will carry	apajjá	apa + jjá
I carry (it) for you	apt'arapsmawa	ap+ t'a + rapi + sma+ wa
Please carry (it) for me	apt'arapitalla	ap + t'a + rapi + ta + lla

Nouns also have suffixes:

Father	auqui
My father	auquijja
Your father	auquima
His father	auquipa
Our father	auquisa

During my period of using canned homilies and ceremonial texts, I made some terrible mistakes. For example, in the wedding ceremony, there is a ritual admonition to remind the new couple of the seriousness of marriage and the importance of being compatible. Within the admonition is the advice for the couple not to argue for no reason or insult each other. The phrase was *Jan aynisimpti*. In my faulty pronunciation, I missed by one sound and was telling them not to have sexual relations. What kept the groom from hitting me, or the couple simply guffawing in mid-ceremony was a sign of extreme respect. The sacristan simply turned around to hide his laughing quietly or biting his tongue. I was struggling. With my flimsy grasp of Aymara, I wrote out short sermons until I could gain some fluency in the language.

I spent three months at the Maryknoll Language School in Cochabamba, Bolivia. All the classes were one-on-one instruction. We attended four one-hour classes with four different instructors. The variety of instructors helped us distinguish the individual differences in the spoken language. The afternoon was spent in listening to tapes in the language lab as a way of getting used to hearing the language. The evening was spent in preparing for the next day's four live sessions with our instructors. We simply had to be ready for the drills, the speaking and actual communicating.

I finally was able to correct many bad habits I had developed in my attempt to learn Aymara. When I finished the language-learning course, I was more expressive in Aymara than I had been up to that point. I could write out longer sermons. When I had finished with Sunday Masses, I began writing the following Sunday's sermon. I practiced the sermon at daily Mass, made corrections after each Mass until I was ready with an effective sermon the following Sunday. I talked with people in the villages and in town, but I still spoke with some difficulty. One time when I was addressing a group of villagers, the women in the group said as I finished, "You speak like a baby. It's fun to talk with you." I never suffered for a lack of critics. Nonetheless, I felt more confident in addressing and conversing with people. When I did not make myself clear, people would say: "We do not speak English. Why do you talk to us in English?" I still had a long way to go. Success was in practicing daily, so, I didn't stop talking.

While I was at language school, Ilave got a new pastor, Fr. Joe, along with two other priests and a Maryknoll Brother. Joe was very different from the previous two pastors. He was very critical of previous parish policies, particularly celebrating Mass so freely when people had no understanding of Mass. His criticism was aimed more directly at the celebration of fiesta Masses in the haciendas of the local townspeople and in the *estancias*. He stopped the practice of Fiesta Masses in the villages and in town and the use of saint statues. He wanted the people to understand the Mass before he would celebrate it indiscriminately. Joe apparently was very much in touch with the directives coming from the Second Vatican Council regarding the Mass:

> The Church, therefore, earnestly desires that Christ's faithful, when present at this mystery of faith, should not be there as strangers or silent spectators; on the contrary, through a good

understanding of the rites and prayers they should take part in the sacred action, conscious of what they are doing, with devotion and collaboration.[6]

In the traditional view of mission, clergy mostly went to people who had not heard of Christ and his message. In places where people had already been evangelized, the missioners were to provide pastoral care to the people. Joe had just added another dimension to the practice of mission when he assigned catechists to attend to the villages with prayer services instead of Mass. Joe's move reflected the concepts I had drawn from Roland Allen's books on establishing the church and moving on with the responsibility of the growth of the church in the hands of new converts. However, the strong reason for limiting Masses, in Joe's mind, was the imminent scarcity of priests, maybe even none, to care for the people. He wanted to force the townspeople to resolve the problem of very few priests, very likely of no priests. As far as I could tell, he did not consult with the catechists or the townspeople on the suspension of Masses in villages and limited Masses in town. Based on what the catechists had done in the past, he assigned them to conduct prayer services and gave them the title of lay pastors. I sensed both his lack of pastoral care and the limited training of the catechists troubling as this vision veered drastically from establishing the church and leaving it in the hands of new converts.

While Joe was restructuring the pastoral agenda of the parish, my new assignment was to study Clinical Pastoral Education (CPE) in New York. CPE is an intensely supervised pastoral training in a hospital setting aimed at developing professional skills in spiritual care. The training consisted of ministry through a process of reflection and action and was open to clergy and seminarians of all faiths working together as an interfaith community. The setting contributed to defining mission and missionary work: namely, the spiritual care of all people regardless of religious affiliation. I was to study at the old Lutheran Hospital in Brooklyn, New York, under the supervision of Rev. Robert Cholke, a Lutheran pastor from the New York Synod. The members of my group consisted of two Lutheran seminarians, two Anglican seminarians and myself. Our tasks were to minister to people in crisis, such as during hospitalization. Each of us was to follow a patient from the time of admission and their time under treatment, including surgery; we accompanied him or her as they underwent anesthesia, the actual operation, recovery, and finally, we visited and interacted with him or her up to the time of release from the hospital. We were to listen to the patient's concerns during their stay and keep track of our responses to that person. Afterwards,

6. Paul VI, "*Sacrosanctum*," no. 48:

we wrote and presented a verbatim report of this pastoral encounter and related our own response to visiting, observing and interviewing the patient. These visits were not data gathering but a review of our ministering to persons facing a crisis in their lives.

Afterwards, we all met with Cholke to present our report for feedback; in the give and take critique, we developed a new awareness of ourselves as persons and as pastors. We also became keenly aware of the spiritual needs of the people whom we pastored. The discussion flowed quite naturally into a theological reflection applicable to all human situations. It is interesting to note that the reflection of this sort did not focus on the differences of the faiths or theologies, but on the needs of the patients. In this setting, a minister really hears his people and assesses their spiritual needs, thereby, dropping any preconceived ideas about the patient. Likewise, we understood that no textbook answers resolve people's problems, that we see and accept people as they are, not as we would like to see them. We learned to distance ourselves from "my learning, my knowledge about these things, my notions of pain" to hearing what a patient says. We saw that, from the patient's being heard, he/she underwent a healing of its own kind. This is really a thorough understanding of ministry, not as the observation and admonition of a distant observer but a personal encounter with people in critical need. Jesus did the same when he mingled with taxpayers, sinners and prostitutes who needed him. CPE helped us find our self-identity in ministry and in the spiritual care of individuals, families, and our churches. This training put ministry into a real-life profession that influences and affects people's lives.

While Bob Cholke gave me an excellent review when I finished CPE training, I learned a new perspective on mission. Moreover, Bob liked the fact that I worked with native communities and was somewhat familiar with Aymara religious customs. He asked me to gather material on natural sacrament, namely those ceremonies and actions people use to make them aware of God's presence and blessing; together we would write up a theology of sacrament based on these observations. This task got me charged to bring together theological, psychological and pastoral insights into my work. But this project was secondary; more importantly, CPE taught me to define mission as listening and hearing the needs presented to us as spiritual leaders. CPE had a definite effect on me. My role was not to continue from a position of privilege and authority, certainly not the idol crusher that I had originally thought would be my mission. My new skills consisted of determining the spiritual needs of people without their having to meet certain conditions before I would minister to them. They were people, children of God who loves them far more than I could ever love them.

3

The Spiritual Life of the Aymara

Jesus said to him, "What do you want me to do for you?"

"Master, I want to see."

—Mark 10: 51

After the CPE training, I bought a Pentax camera to record the religious practices of the Aymara since Cholke had asked me to collect data on natural sacrament. While I was excited about this new project, I returned to Peru with a certain trepidation. The Sisters in Ilave had been writing regularly to me during my time in New York. They felt abandoned because Joe, the new pastor, appeared to have eliminated the pastoral care of the parishioners. The traditional service with Mass and the sacraments was slipping away and they wondered what would replace it.

I tried to fit into the pastoral framework that Joe was implementing with fewer Masses and the sacraments, but we still had to recognize the sentiments of the people. My recent training in Clinical Pastoral Education defined for me the task of ministering more directly, more personally, and more professionally rather than in a routine-like practice. I found myself torn between attending to the people's requests and following the new policy of the parish. People were still coming in large numbers for baptism and they continued to ask for Masses and blessings for their saints which they dressed in velvet robes with silver trim to "hear the Mass." Those practices did not change in the face of Joe's policy of reduced traditional ministry. I asked myself: What are the spiritual needs of the people and how can we be in touch with them? Would denying Masses for them convince people to conform to our concept of a Catholic lifeway? Would they change? I felt I had a long way to go to find the right answers to these questions.

However, in response to the Sisters' and the townspeople's complaints, I continued with traditional Masses and visits to the sick. I supported the Sisters in their pastoral activities, praying with them in visits to the sick. The Sisters often asked me to celebrate Mass for them at the convent as they were never sure there would even be a Mass at the church. It made me happy to grant them their requests because it was for their spiritual needs, and it was uplifting for me.

An example of how spiritual enrichment affected me happened when I had accompanied the Sisters on a picnic. We went to a bend in the river across from the town of Ilave, just as people were bringing their animals for water. Everyone was excited to be out. The weather was beautiful, sunny and warm, and the river glistened in the sun. A man brought his donkey and ox to the river's edge to drink water. Two other people were leading their donkeys loaded with *llima*, river grass that served as feed for the animals at home. The small sparrow-like birds flew low to the ground. I remember how everyone was so happy: the nuns, the man with his animals, and the women who washed the llima of dirt and mud. Even the donkey and the ox seemed happy with their water. I felt almost giddy with this wonderfully beautiful scene. As we sat down to eat, one of the Sisters, Barbara, asked me to give thanks. I was so transfixed by this joyful moment. I took a Bible, opened it as if guided to Psalm 104, 10–15.

> You make springs flow into channels
> that wind among the mountains.
> They give drink to every beast of the field;
> Here wild asses quench their thirst.
> Beside them the birds of heaven nest;
> Among the branches they sing.
> You water the mountains from your palace;
> By your labor the earth abounds.
> You raise grass for the cattle
> And plants for our beasts of burden.
> You bring bread from the earth
> and wine to gladden our hearts. . .

All I remember was how that inspiration of the moment filled me with awe, and that memory has stayed with me for years. That was the kind of ministry I wanted to project to a people who had a different concept of religion with fiestas, saints, and dancing. But Joe had already assigned the catechists to perform all the baptisms, make visits to the sick, and perform prayer services in place of fiesta Masses. They were given the title of lay pastors who were to carry out the ministries that priests were no longer performing.

Once, I monitored the catechists as they baptized new babies; I was shocked when I heard them using as sacramental words: "Sutichsmawa. . . . Dios Auqui, Dios Yoka, Dios Espíritu Santo" "I give you the name. . . . in the name of the Father and of the Son and of the Holy Spirit)."

I stopped them and told them that they were not baptizing with those words. I told them that they had to use the words "I baptize you, bautismawa, in the name of the Father and of the Son and of the Holy Spirit. Otherwise it was not baptizing that you are doing." I reported my findings to the other priests but no one appeared to be as upset as I was. Joe was in charge of the catechists and met regularly with them and I do not know if he retrained them to baptize correctly. I questioned whether these baptisms were even valid but none of the priests seemed concerned about my objection. I did not think that the catechists should baptize when the priests were present, neither should we refuse to celebrate Mass as was our duty to do so. With these new pastoral procedures, I felt frustrated and began drifting away from celebrating Mass and administering the sacraments. At Easter, Joe ordered me to go on vacation. I objected since it was a particularly solemn time for me to assist them, but he insisted and ordered me to go. I chose to travel to Ayacucho because of its renowned celebration of Holy Week. To this day, I do not understand why my absence was requested, especially at Easter with its heavily attended Holy Week ceremonies.

In spite of our efforts, there was no indication of a change in the people's religiosity any time soon, or ever. The people still came to the church, especially to baptize their children. My pursuit now involved the question that had haunted me since I had settled into this parish: why do the Aymara, as well as the townspeople, not want to change? Simply asking questions did not offer any answers. This question became more poignant in one particular incident. I had visited Maquera village and was returning home when I noticed a lush potato field with noticeably large potato plants. I simply had to stop and look at these plants. A man happened to be leaning on a field stone fence looking at this same field, so I walked up to him and started a conversation. His name was Francisco. Eventually we talked about the potato plants. I said, "These plants are so high. They must be over a meter high."

"They belong to a *huirajocha* [gentleman] in town," he informed me. Then I pointed to an adjacent field with plants barely a foot high. "They are mine," he told me. "Why are these so tall and yours are so small?" I asked.

"The huirajocha irrigates his plants." he replied. "I don't want to irrigate." I was puzzled why he did not want to irrigate his plants. "You can see that they are much bigger with some irrigation." "Yes, he said, "but it would not be good to take so much from Pachamama (Mother Earth)."

What kind of power did Mother Earth have on the people here? As I was about to question this notion, he said he had to get home. I left too but I kept asking myself why people here did not change, or worse, not want to change. I was not satisfied with the answer about offending Mother Earth.

Other similar questions did not seem to provide an answer to non-change: Why does Aymara still persist as the language of this region in spite of Spanish influence for the last 400 years? Why do people still use the short-handle hoe to harvest potatoes when a spade or garden fork could be more efficient?

When I asked these questions, the answers were always the same: "It will offend Pachamama." Or, "We need to show respect for the potatoes." Some of the answers left me with the impression that it was not good to progress too much, whether in farming, in leaving one's community behind, or in accumulating wealth. A bumper crop appeared to threaten the meaning of Mother Earth's goodness, and this source of life could turn on the people and demand retribution. Whatever innovation in farming one would introduce had little or no positive effect if it involved antagonizing Mother Earth.

Even wealth was seen in the context of Mother Earth. It appears that people need to share their wealth. When a person prospers, whether in farming or in business, he is named to sponsor the year's fiesta in honor of the saint of the community. This saint could be St. Anthony, Santo Niño, Santa Cruz or any other saint. In addition, there are several popular saints, and each village has one or two who are the spiritual keepers of that village. When the feast of these saints comes around, the village has an elaborate party with a hired band, dancers in costume and plenty of food and drink. The villagers look for a person who can sponsor and pay for the greater part of this fiesta. This person is called an *alferado,* usually a man of wealth whose role is chief organizer of the patronal feast; women can be named co-sponsors. He is responsible for the continuation of this massive celebration. For his role, he receives several rewards for his contribution and his status rises to that of elder or leader in that community. He is often made an official of the village as chief, judge or simply an elder with authority, symbolized with a staff or a whip. His word is power.[1]

While he covers most of the expense of this celebration, others are named as godfathers, who contribute money or goods, since this expense can be exorbitant in the face of the limited resources of the village. To me, this kind of celebrating seems to keep people who prosper within the boundaries of acceptance in each village. It allows one to share the wealth and avoid offending the guardian spirits. They believe that offending the spirits can bring havoc to a village, and this belief has a long history among the Aymara. The first missionaries added new fears of offending God as they tried to force Christianity on the Aymara.

I simply had to find out what made the people's motives so strong in maintaining their traditions. I recall that one time I had suggested raising the cooking stove from the floor to a waist high level. The stoves are made of clay about 18 inches high, about thirty inches long and about 18 inches wide, with a hole on the front to feed the fire and two round holes on top for the cooking pots. Since no one liked my idea of a high stove, I asked why it was such a problem, but I never got a direct answer; but over a period of time I found out that women felt cold when they stood. They were able to warm up by sitting in front of the fire. It took a long time before I learned the real reason why women did not want their stoves raised from the floor. If they are reluctant to change something practical, how much harder is it to change religious customs?

The Sunday market provided clues that could tell me why people are persistent in traditional ways. On market days, people congregated to buy and sell, to drink and socialize. One Sunday, I saw some women selling dried llama embryos. When asked what they do with these embryos, they told me that they were for the *anchanchu,* a vampire-like ghost who moves about a village at night and, finding a victim, sucks the fat from the liver. I bought one and brought it to show it to our employees, Domingo and Hipólito. They gave me no explanation but directed me to talk to the men and women who sell ritual supplies in the plaza.

It took me six years to notice for the first time a candy stand that drew no children as customers. I asked the elderly woman, Maria, who sold the candies, how it was that children did not buy these candies. She told me, "People buy these for making sacrifices to Mother Earth, candies for the *dulce misa,* the sweet table."

---

1. Salazar, Unpublished manuscript, October 10, 1971.

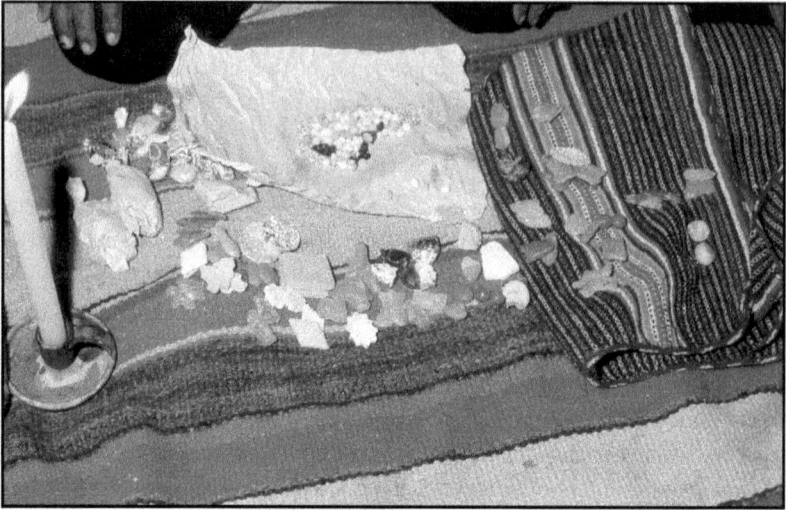

Dulce misa, the sweet table, is a candy offering depicting all the items a family needs for their daily care. Modern "misas" include radios and cars or trucks. The misa is burned as an offering to the achachilas.

This *misa* consisted of animals, houses, trucks, radios and many other figures, some wrapped in gold or silver colored foil. They symbolized the things one needs for everyday life. She also had displays of tiny, quarter inch metal figurines of the same items as depicted in the candies. This smaller offering is called the *ch'iuchi misa,* the little table. She did not elaborate and I let it go at that. Actually, what was in the back of my mind was to buy up these figures and use them to preach against what I regarded as idolatry.

Still, I did not know enough about these sacrifices. I returned to this stand on other Sundays. Finally, I saw some men buying up a bundle of these candies. I stopped to talk to them and asked about their misa for Mother Earth. They were reluctant to tell me anything about their purchase. I told the men I wanted to attend this offering to Mother Earth because I did not understand much of what they do and think and I wanted to learn. Going to one of these ceremonies, I explained, might help me understand.

They responded as if given a cue. They spoke in a deliberately slow and simple Aymara so that I could understand everything they said. First, they spoke among themselves, describing how I had treated them and did not respect what they did in church. They recalled how I had knocked over candles and sometime refused to bless their flowers or kerosene. They could have gone on for a good while about my behavior toward them. Suddenly, they turned toward me and said, "You can come to our misa." They told me the day and time of the gathering and how to get to their village. The men left and I stayed to talk with Maria. Her daughter, also Maria, joined the conversation and assured me that it was a simple all-night ceremony.

I began having second thoughts about this visit because it might involve devil worship; this worry was the result of Catholic prejudices against strange non-Catholic practices. I asked Domingo, the sacristan, and Hipólito, the parish secretary, to accompany me. I told Joe that I was going to a meeting in a local village. Since he had no specific plans or tasks for me, I was pretty much free to do what I wanted. He did not assign me any tasks at all while he was pastor.

In spite of my fears, we still went to the village straight to the house of Simeona Mamani, the beneficiary of this misa. Domingo, Hipólito and I went in and saw that the family had already taken their places. They made no fanfare about our presence and proceeded with the ceremony. Since there was a lot of time for conversing, the *pacco* (shaman) who was officiating this ceremony made comments about us but did not always speak directly to us. There was a second pacco, who was afraid to come in. He felt that we were going to scold him for what he was doing and that his activity was wrong. He knew from experience and from stories of the past how practitioners of the native religion were punished and forced to recant their beliefs and practices. Still, in the face of these punishments, the people continued to make their offerings to Mother Earth.

The ceremony went smoothly but I did not understand any of it. It was too new for me. I asked if I could take pictures and record the session. As I was curious and had a lot of questions, they gave me full permission. There were invocations with coca, a rubbing down of Simeona, the sick woman, with the sacrificial bundle and a lot of prayers with incense. The pacco said he was trying to call back the soul of the sick woman. He addressed several spirits to see which one had stolen her soul. Children were most vulnerable to losing their souls to these local spirits.

At this time, I had a sketchy understanding of the Aymara spirit world. In traditional story-telling, the principle deity is the Sun, *Inti,* who watches the world from his position in the sky. People address him as *Tatitu Inti* or Father Sun. His consort, *Paksi,* the moon, addressed as *Mamita Paksi,* watches over the world at night. Because of the concern shown by these two deities, people see the sun and the moon as compassionate gods. In the Tiahuanaco ruins, the sun is depicted as shedding tears for the people. Since the Sun is so far away and does not have direct contact with the people, he has as messenger the condor that flies so high that he can talk to the Sun. When the condor comes to earth, he perches on the mountaintops, the grandfathers, the *achachilanaca,* to convey to them the messages from the sun. These mountain spirits originated from the age of darkness.

The catechists told me all these stories, especially about a time before there was light, that giant creatures inhabited the earth in darkness and possessed a variety of powers that now control people's lives and the forces of nature. At some point, they committed some error or sin. The Sun came out of the middle of Lake Titicaca and, as punishment, froze all those giants into stones, hills and mountains, according to their place in the hierarchy in the world of darkness. A good example of these formations is the place called Ciudad Encantada, the Enchanted City. At first, I thought these stories about giants were to scare children but, in later research, I sensed that they were part of the creation stories passed on as the origin of the Incas.[2]

In every home, there is a large stone in the middle of the patio. It is called *huaca kala,* the old stone, referring to the huacas, the ancient local spirits. According to Garcilaso de la Vega's *Comentarios Reales de los Incas, Huaca* signifies an idol in its first meaning, but it is also equivalent to a sacred object with an indwelling spirit and is then applied to crags, stones, trees, springs and other natural formations.[3] In private homes, this stone is often used as a hitching post for a cow or donkey without losing its status as huaca. For that task, the stone is called a *picota.*

From this partial scenario of the spirit world, one can understand how anthropologists have described the Aymara as fatalistic pessimists. Their whole world is dominated by a multitude of spirits and magic, and they become victims of their own belief system. Nonetheless, they have the techniques and rituals to overcome any menacing hold these spirits may have over them. These are the rites known as *salud misa, katjja misa, ch'iuchi misa, and cuti misa* among others. These offerings with their respective ceremony keep a person from falling into an extreme despair since these rites work for them and remove illnesses or curses.

The Spanish conquistadors and the missionaries who accompanied them saw the native religion as erroneous and immediately initiated efforts to eradicate it; Padre Pablo José de Arriaga developed a precise plan to eliminate what he believed was idolatry. From his lengthy descriptions of the religious practices which he gleaned from interrogating the sorcerers and their followers, I realized that I had photographed many of those same practices Arriaga described in his book. For example, Arriaga identifies *mullu* as scallop shells.[4] *Mullu* are also the stone figures that were rubbed

2. Cobo, *History,* pp. 94–97.

3. Garcilaso, p. 20.

4. Arriaga, *Extirpation,* p. 43.

with gold and silver because the *mullu* itself is the spirit depicted. I have one that has traces of the silver still showing on the base of the mullu. Many of the mullu stones in my collection are gifts from several shamans.

Author's collection of Aymara mullu figures. Most are gifts from local yatiri.

One characteristic of these figures is that they are not square but trapezoidal in shape. Arriaga also refers to the sacrifice made up of small figures probably made of quinoa paste; this is called dulce misa today.[5] One major reason for offering a salud misa is that the spirits readily become angry with the people and the believers placate these spirits with a salud misa. This kind of offering is beneficial for the participants and is called white magic.

An offering to seek revenge is called Cuti Misa, or black magic. The injured party turns the offender over to Mother Earth who will swallow him up. This kind of ritual lets the followers seek revenge without taking time out to fight in a feud that could last for generations.

In all the rites, the yatiri asks all present to confess their wrongs and to reconcile with their family members. Arriaga also describes the confession that the sorcerer requires of the participants in these rites. This confession of wrongs is still carried out with an offering of incense in a bowl, and the participants embrace each other and ask for forgiveness for the offenses committed among themselves. Without a true confession, the offering will not be effective and misfortune could befall the whole group.

5. Arriaga, *Extirpation*, p.75.

There are no frightful or hideous idols to scare people into submission; however, many spirits are ambivalent. They can bless a person or family with good crops and a good life, or a spirit can take a soul captive, thereby blocking one from attaining these benefits. As for idols, Arriaga describes one figure as an abominable stone idol with the male side facing the rising sun.[6] It was located two leagues or about six miles from the town of Ilave. After having looked for this site for nearly two years, I discovered it. I had visited several villages within two leagues from town before discovering it in the village of Compuyo. This village was the likely site because the hillside facing the present-day road was a natural slope facing the road. On the village side, the same hill had a flat area as if a platform had been cut into the hill. I asked if any statue had ever existed there. The villagers took me to a stone fence where the statue was used as part of the fence. It was really a stela with the male figure on one side and supposedly, a female on the other. The male side had the genital area chipped away but the female's body was completely chipped away. We pulled the stela out, cleaned it, and I took photographs, but my photos were lost. Scattered about were a number of stones in block form with sexual symbols. At carnival, the villagers dance around all these stone figures.

After observing the first ceremony for Simeona Mamani, I returned to Maria's candy stand several Sundays with many questions. She answered some of them, as I tried to find out why people adhered to the old ways. The best yatiri that she knew was Marcelino; he would help me understand. I met him one Sunday by Maria's kiosk. She told Marcelino that I wanted to know the people better and that perhaps my attending the misa, also called *pago* ceremony, would help me understand. He agreed to have me come to the salud misa he was going to conduct the following Wednesday.

Marcelino is a blind shaman from the village of Jach'a Winch'occa, 12 miles southwest of Lake Titicaca. He was 38 years old when I first met him. His village was close to Ilave. He was both a healer and a diviner and had served as cantor at the local church. At a misa in the village of Simillaca, Marcelino told us how he lost his sight and become aware of his calling as a yatiri. Some eighteen years back, he became extremely ill. He told me how his eyes had become very black and shiny. His breath was a wet rattle and he was very hot to the touch. His family saw no other remedy but to have him bled. They took him to a medicine man named Isidro, who cut two incisions with glass shards in several spots at the forehead just above the hairline. He bled a steady flow for a while until the bleeding stopped. His hair stood up stiff from the dried blood. He slept for a good while, and

6. Arriaga, *Extirpation*, p. 75.

when he awoke, he could not see. Marcelino said that he tried other medicine men and even went to the hospital. They all told him he was crazy. There was no cure for him.

Eventually, he realized that he had escaped death; and because he had been spared, he was to be a yatiri. God had called him to help and to heal others. He could read coca leaves by touching them; he could tell a person's need by listening to them. He was able to discern the loss of a soul. In his role of performing healing ceremonies, he was able to call back lost souls and to heal people of many other maladies.[7]

The following Wednesday evening, I went to Jamach'oco village for the salud misa to heal a little boy. "Mant'malla (Come in)" Marcelino told us. I entered the adobe home and took my place in the circle. The room was dimly lit with just two candles. Shadows danced behind each of us as the flames flickered. The ceremony was simple and long, lasting until dawn the next day.

The sick child, Pedrito, was in his mother's arms. His eyes were half closed, his lips parched from his fever, and his face was flushed and tear stained. His parents, Rufino and Lucia, were seated to the left of Marcelino. Immediately next to Marcelino was his wife, Asunta. She coached and directed Marcelino throughout the ritual activity.

The rest of the family sat in a circle on the dirt floor. They used ponchos, blankets, or sheepskins as ground covers. Everyone was conversing in soft voices. Marcelino took the baby in his arms and rocked him for a bit and the baby fell asleep. He told Lucia to lay the baby on the bed and asked her to get him some clothes the baby wears. Marcelino took them and shaped them into a makeshift doll and laid it between him and the ceremonial blanket.

Marcelino acknowledged my presence by telling stories about the hill spirits and the mountains, about the origins of the people and about the way of healing. Marcelino elaborated on the particular spirits that "make a person ill." Besides the mountains and hills, there are lesser spirits in this hierarchy. There are *pujuni*, the female spirits or sirens, who live in springs and water holes. Certain boulders are good spirits; others are evil. A house has several spirits. There are the *uyhuiri*, the watchman, and the *utani*, the owner of the house. These spirits rank low in the hierarchy and are most vulnerable to the scheming of a greater and possibly evil spirit, a *supaya*, translated as devil. Even dirt devils or dust spirals are known there as supaya or *tutuka*. A supaya can inquire from the house spirit all he wants to know about its resident. The utani, in particular, is weak and gives all the

7. Salazar, Unpublished Transcript, May 12, 1971, pp.1–2.

information the *supaya* wants. The spirits apparently communicate among themselves in order to maintain control of their subjects.[8]

Churches and the bells of the church also have similar spirits and can inadvertently give information about the people who attend that church. There are many other spirits, but the list is too long to describe here, since most of them are linked to places like hills and waterholes. All these spirits, whose origin is from the age of darkness, are the ones who inflict illnesses on children and adults for no apparent reason other than the whim of that spirit. This is how he began to educate me.

Marcelino proceeded to lay out the ritual elements on the incuña, a square 30-inch cloth woven into two broad bands decorated with multicolored stripes on both sides of each wide band. Immediately, I could sense the smell of sage, coca leaves, incense, and llama fat. All turned their attention to Marcelino as he began the healing ceremony, by asking for a burning brazier and incense. He sprinkled incense on the burning coals and prayed, then invoked the achachilas, adding incense and asking pardon of all the local spirits and places (uyhuiri, utani, pujuni) for his intrusion into their area. He addressed each spirit by name, and repeated the litany of spirits and invocations in the name of each member of the family; he proceeded with a confession of his own wrongdoings and asked pardon for all present and for absent members of the family. He passed the brazier to the participants for each to confess wrongdoings and to ask pardon personally of the spirits and of each other. As each person confessed in a semi-audible voice and with sighs of repentance, Marcelino prayed parts of the Lord' prayer, probably to give the ceremony a semblance of Christian practice.

My strongest impression at that moment was how much at home I was with this family and how readily Marcelino accepted me into this circle that belonged only to the Aymara. This was the first of many visits to the ceremonies Marcelino performed. I had begun a dialogue with another religion, which was not at all Catholic.

The service was done in four stages: first, the "dulce misa," followed by the "*apostol misa*" that takes its name from the twelve rows of twelve coca leaf triads, called *q'intus*, for a total of 144 triads. (fig. 13)

---

8. Salazar, Unpublished Transcript, May 13, 1971.

Apostle misa, 12 rows of 3 leaf bundles called qintu, represent the major local spirits. They appear during the ceremony to offer advice about the family's problems.

The twelve rows are called apostles, likely, to hide the native practice with names learned from the first Catholic missionaries. These twelve apostles are really the principal hill spirits that dominate the area where this offering is being conducted. All of the spirits near the offering site have to be invoked because all know something about the family, especially about the sick person. Marcelino consulted with these spirits in the third stage of this rite. Everyone had to extinguish candles and lamps as the spirits came in total darkness, swishing and fanning through the air; even I felt the rush of air as the spirit passed by me. We all felt their presence. They greeted Marcelino and each of the participants and quickly proceeded to give instructions to Marcelino and the family in gruff, authoritative voices; then they left as suddenly as they had arrived.

Once the candles were relit, Marcelino interpreted the coca, scattered about on the ritual cloth by the visiting spirits; the interpretation consisted of specific instructions on how each member of the family was to behave toward each other and what to expect for their good conduct.

The last stage involved the burning of the sacrificial bundle in the patio or a designated sacred spot. Afterwards, the men slaughtered a black sheep and Marcelino sprinkled the participants and the house with the blood of the sheep.

When the ceremony was over, we sat around for the exact time to call back Pedrito's soul. At about two in the morning, Marcelino sat up and said, "It is time to call the soul." There was no noise at all. Not even the dogs in the village barked. Marcelino picked up the doll he had made and a small bell. He said, "Animojj jak'achatawa" (The soul is close by). He went out the door with no help from anyone. With the doll in one arm and the bell in the other hand, he stepped out and went out to the edge of the stone corral surrounding the house. He faced one-way and then another. He seemed to fix his gaze in one direction and began speaking to the soul to come back. He told the soul, "We all miss you, Pedrito." He rang the bell gently so that it made a soft tinkle. "Come back, Pedrito, come back," he kept saying, as he started walking backwards to the door of the house. All the while he kept calling the soul by name and ringing the bell. Marcelino backed his way in through the door directly to the bed where Pedrito was sleeping. He touched the baby with the makeshift doll; Pedrito jumped in his sleep as if startled. He did not wake-up but slept peacefully with the doll next to him. Marcelino told the family to give the child something to eat in the morning. Marcelino, his wife and I prepared to leave. We saw the child, who was sleeping calmly, no longer restless and agitated.

I had just witnessed a genuine healing. It was enough to make one a believer. Marcelino attended to people in their needs. He had the ability to solve their problems and heal their ills according to their beliefs. He did not force people to believe one way or another. He did not threaten or punish. Arriaga prohibited this ritual of the salud misa because the person cured would return to idolatry.[9]

When I walked out the door with Marcelino, I emerged with a new soul and a new way of seeing the Aymara people. Here is a person who is moved by spirit and heals. This is the same Spirit I believe in who enlightens, guides and heals. Otherwise I would have to say that there are other spirits in the various religions who also guide and heal. I had been blind and now I saw, thanks to Marcelino. My faith in people burst open and blossomed. I wanted to tell everyone about the real Aymara. I lost that notion that what I believe is correct and what others believe is wrong. This is the Spirit working through sincere and simple persons, not through orthodoxy and established teachings. This insight cast me into a new role as a spokesman for the Aymara people and for all native peoples and their spiritual life.

I took my colleagues to these ceremonies. Father Domingo, an Aymara, went with me on several occasions. He began writing quite a bit on the Aymara culture, now that he had the opportunity to observe his own

9. Arriaga, *Extirpation,* p. 79.

culture. His family were members of the Adventist Church and did not practice these rituals. He was from the village of Socca on the shores of Lake Titicaca near the town of Acora. He chose to become a Catholic and, once baptized, he was recruited to study for the priesthood; the bishop sent him to the diocesan seminary in Boston, Massachusetts, where he spent his formative years away from his native surroundings and did not return to Peru until his ordination at age 25.

These ceremonies he saw with me gave him a new picture of the cultural expressions he had missed. I also invited the Sisters from Ilave and the Sisters from the neighboring parish to observe these rites. Joe even accompanied me to see the *ch'utas*, a daybreak ceremony performed on the feast of Pentecost. He had to make the sacrifice of getting up at the first light of dawn. I even took Bobby Kennedy, Jr. to a salud misa. Bobby spent a summer with us on the recommendation of Fr. Miguel D'Escoto, a Maryknoller who had worked in Chile and was the founder of Orbis Books, Maryknoll's publishing arm. Observing the Aymara rites was not solely my project and mine alone. I wanted everyone to get to know the Aymara as they really are, a deeply spiritual people. All of this effort certainly fit into the spirit of the Vatican II document: Declaration on the relation of the church to non-Christian religions, *Nostra Aetate*:

> In our time, when day by day mankind is being drawn closer together, and the ties between different peoples are becoming stronger, the Church examines more closely her relationship to non-Christian religions. In her task of promoting unity and love among men, indeed among nations, she considers above all in this declaration what men have in common and what draws them to fellowship.[10]

There were a number of other sacred ceremonies that I observed. At the village of Chillacollo, the people gathered to perform a misa for the first plowing as they readied the fields for sowing the crops. They made offerings to the local spirits and especially to those of wind, hail and frost. This rite is based on one of the myths from the age of darkness. Pedro Copaja, a deeply dedicated catechist, told me the tale of three brothers from the age of darkness who lived with their widowed mother. She told them that they had to work hard and plant a new crop as they were almost out of food. They took some seed potatoes and set out to work.

But they were young and irresponsible and spent their time playing; they even cooked the seed potatoes their mother had given them to plant. When they returned home, tired and dirty, their mother fixed them a meal.

10. Pope Paul VI, *Nostra Aetate*, p. 57.

She had them rest, as they were surely tired from the fieldwork. She sent them out again at different times to tend to the potato fields; but the three brothers spent their time playing, each time coming home tired but not from work. Then, the mother sent them to put more soil on the plants and to weed the field.

When harvest time arrived, the boys did not know what to do, as they had no crop. They said, "Let's steal from the neighbors." They brought home big loads of potatoes. The mother was so proud of them that she cooked a bigger batch of potatoes. While the pot was on the fire, the angry neighbors came and practically knocked down the door they were so furious. They told the mother that her sons were lazy and had never planted any potatoes. They took their potatoes back, even the ones that were cooking. The mother was so upset. "What can I give my children?" she cried. She then took a knife and cut a large piece of muscle from her thigh. She cooked it, fed her sons, and, inevitably, bled to death.

The sons were filled with rage, as they had no one to care for them. One said, "We will get those stingy neighbors. I will be *thaya*, wind. I will blow and blow until all the plants lose their blossoms and not give any potatoes." He went off to the mountaintop as the spirit of the wind. The next brother said, "I will be *juyphi* (frost) and I will freeze the plants so that they cannot produce anything." The last brother said, "I will be *chhijjchi* (hail). Whatever is standing I will crush with my hail and nothing will be left, only ice filled water flowing green from the crushed plants." They went off to the mountaintops to be the spirits of wind, frost, and hail.

That was the kind of harmful power attributed to the creatures from the age of darkness who are now hill spirits. People believed they had to placate them with this misa to protect their crops from the devastating elements. Once performed, the people could proceed with preparing the soil for the sowing. It was not at all ironic that one of our chief catechists was the director for this ritual procedure, since the catechists were the principal informants of these stories. The catechists acted as if it was most natural for me to be there with them.

The procedure was much like the salud misa mentioned above except that it was done for the whole community, in daylight and at the farm field being readied for sowing. The men officiated at the ceremony, but the women participated by offering coca leaf *q'intus* (three leaves of coca held with the thumb and forefinger) held close to the mouth to invoke the various spirits of the area.

After the ceremony, the women laid out a row of *llijjllas*, the large wool square blankets used for carrying babies and large bundles on their backs. They served boiled potatoes on these blankets. We all sat down to eat. Some women picked the best potatoes and brought them to me. The catechist sat by me and asked me what I thought of the ceremony. I told him that I was impressed. After a very brief conversation, he got up and left.

After lunch, the men hitched a pair of oxen to a yoke for the first plowing. They made some invocations and sprinkled the ground with alcohol made from sugar cane. They proceeded to make one row of plowed earth. They all gathered and drank some alcohol before continuing to plow. I left as they continued drinking.

Fr. Phillip, the pastor from a neighboring parish, told me that his catechists had given up the native rites. He claimed that these customs no longer existed in his parish. I challenged him to pick a village of his choice that we could visit on Pentecost day. Pentecost marked the end of the harvest when people celebrated the feast with a smoking of the fields. They cleaned the fields of all plants and made small smoking fires all around the fields. There was no flame to the fires but a low hanging smoke. These fires were called *ch'utas*.

Ch'utas are flameless fires whose smoke floats close to the ground over newly harvested fields. They are lit on Pentecost Sunday in thanksgiving for the new crops. Every field is honored and the whole countryside in covered in smoke.

Everyone came out to tend the fires so that they simply let off smoke over the fields. It was a way of honoring the fields for the crop they had yielded. People commented how beautiful this smoke looked. "It's like the Spirit has come over the land."

On that day, Phil and I drove to the village of his head catechist. As we went over a small hill onto the plain where this village stood, we could see the smoke from the offerings covering the whole plain. We drove to the catechist's house. He was completely engrossed in the ritual and became embarrassed that he had been caught. The pastor was ready to scold him, but I asked the catechist, how was his harvest? He said, "It has been a wonderful harvest. We are so happy and we thank Mother Earth with these ch'utas." The pastor was dumbfounded that his head catechist and outstanding Christian was performing these rites.

Another custom related to the potato takes place at Carnival, also called Mardi Gras in other countries, the three days before Ash Wednesday and the beginning of Lent. The Spanish used to dance and party before Lent began. Since they observed the forty days of Lent with fasting and penance, this fiesta was a last fling before those painful forty days. But for the Aymara, it was a party to commemorate the origin of the potato.[11]

The potato is the main staple of this region. Potatoes originated in the Andes and with the Spanish conquest made their way into Europe. Pedro Cieza de León in his *Crónica del Peru* documents potatoes for the first time as they were unknown to Europeans.[12] In 1565 Gonzalo Jiménez de Quesada took potatoes to Spain. He did not find gold but he did start the supply of potatoes to Spain. He also noticed that the sailors who ate potatoes did not get scurvy.

In the area where I lived, there were 42 different kinds of potatoes, each with its own color, texture and taste; and each was prepared and served in different forms.

At carnival, everyone dances for the potatoes so that they will be happy. They dig up a few potatoes and lay them out on incuñas if they were sacred items. The people sprinkled these choice potatoes with wine and confetti. They encircled the potatoes with streamers and kept them in a prominent place. They consume these special potatoes throughout the year by adding one to each meal on a special occasion.

This practice goes back to another myth from the age of darkness. There were three young girls who went from village to village. At some villages, the elders scolded them severely for going about without a chaperone. "What will your parents say? How do you dare go out like this? You should be punished." All these criticisms made the girls cry. Their giant tears salted the earth, and no crops grew there. At other villages, the people were more

---

11. Salazar, Unpublished Transcripts, p. 3.]
12. Cieza de Leon, *The Discovery*, p. 304.

receptive. "Oh, you poor girls. You look tired. Come and rest. Come, have some tea (junt'uma) to drink." The girls took a seat and drank quietly.

"Can we get you anything else?" the giant villagers asked.

"We are hungry. Can you give us some food?"

The people immediately cooked some food and served the girls. "Is there anything else we can give you?' they asked. The girls sighed and said, "We are so sad. Can you play music for us?"

The people pulled out their flutes and drums, put on dancing costumes and played and danced for the girls with all their heart. As nightfall came, the villagers told the girls that it was time to rest. They all had work the next day and needed to sleep. They gave the girls a room to sleep in. The villagers told them, "When you get up in the morning, you can continue your journey." All went to bed.

The next morning, everyone was up early except the three girls. Everyone thought they were too tired and let them rest a bit longer. After a while, there was still no sign of them. Two men went up to the door of their room but heard nothing. They knocked and still no answer. Gently they pushed the door open only to find three potatoes, three *imillanaca* (little girls), a name given to the potato.

That's how the potato came miraculously to the people who repeatedly told me that the only way to make the potatoes happy is to dance for them. Carnival is the feast recalling the birth of the potato. All have to give the potatoes a place of honor, give them wine and confetti, and most importantly, dance for them. All the weavings incorporate this myth. The broad area of the incuña, the llijllas and ponchos represent the potato fields. The narrow bands of colored stripes represent the dancers and the speckles among these colors are other decorations for the potato.

Once I celebrated a Mass at a village at Carnival time. About two hundred meters in front of the open tent for the altar was a potato field. After Mass as I was taking off the Mass vestments, the people asked me join them in the dance for the potatoes. I had seen one field in front of me and said, "Yes." The music started almost immediately. A man and a woman pulled me into the line of dancers. We danced around the field I had seen from the altar and thought, "Good, we're done." The line moved on to another field and to another and to another. We danced an hour straight without stopping. I was winded from the activity at that altitude but I was not allowed to drop out of the dance line. When we finished, I dropped to the ground and lay there to get my breath. People kept coming up to me, saying, "Thank you, Padre, the potatoes are so happy."

Another ritual involved a lightning strike. It happened in the village of Mortini. I was helping the Sisters with a youth rally at the parish clinic compound when Domingo, the sacristan, came with an urgent message. You have to see this," he told me. "The people of Mortini feel they are going to die. Come quickly."

I told the nuns I had an urgent call and left. They became angry that I would leave them, as this was their first successful youth rally. I assured them they would do well without me and simply left them with all those teenagers. Even though they were upset with me, they were my strongest supporters in my study of the local religion. Sister Jewell made use of my findings in her classes at the local girls' high school and later in Louisiana after her mission in Peru. In her classes, the students discussed how to encourage each other to express their Catholic values as openly as the Aymara so compellingly express their religion.

Meanwhile in Mortini, the villagers had gathered outside the house where the lightning bolt had hit. The people were quiet and frightened. They looked intensely at the shaman who was praying quietly in front of the house. He offered his prayers with a bowl of burning incense. As we walked about among the people, Domingo guided me along with comments on the ongoing activity. We went into the room where the lightning bolt had hit. A blanket covered a small wooden crate that served as an altar for the village saints and some burning candles. On one side of the altar was a large cross with a dead owl stretched out as if crucified. Domingo informed me that the owl was a symbol of death and when shown to the people, this owl would drive away the threat of death.

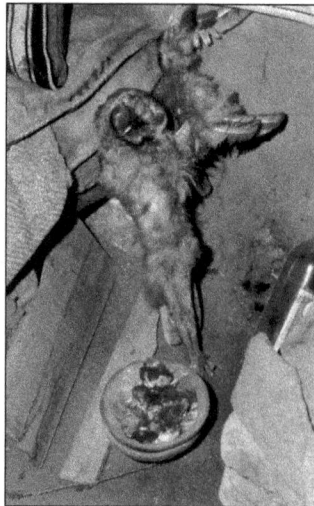

Crucified owl used to ward off death after a lightning strike.

For every ritual I observed, Domingo was intensely dedicated to my learning the Aymara way of life.

The catechist from the village and another man led twelve children, six boys and six girls into the room. They were about eight to ten years old and they represented the twelve apostles. The men led them in prayer as they prayed aloud. They sang some hymns and prayed some more until dawn. The shaman came in, took up the crucified owl outside and we went with him. He held it up high for all to see. The villagers were thus saved from the threat of death. The gesture reminded me of Moses when he raised the bronze serpent to save the Hebrews from death by snake bites as related in Numbers 21, 9.

> Moses accordingly made a bronze serpent and mounted it on
> a pole, and whenever anyone who had been bitten by a serpent
> looked at the bronze serpent, he recovered."

After the shaman raised the owl up above the people, the catechists led the child-apostles outside and we all prayed again. The shaman said in a loud voice, "May this be a good hour." With that the children hugged each other and the people approached them, hugging the children and each other while asking for pardon. This ceremony differed from others because it signified escaping death from Santiago, the hurler of lightning bolts. In describing the beliefs around lightning, Bertonio links *puisakha, Illapa Santiago* as thunder and lightning. In another entry, he describes *Illaphuta* as, "sending lightning from heaven is proper to God." (enviar el rayo del cielo, hacer caer, es propio de Dios.)[13]

I observed many other rites not described here, but one that involved me directly was a *rotuchi*, or the first haircut of a four- or five-year-old child. This is one of the practices that Arriaga describes in his *Extirpation of Idolatry in Peru*.

> When the Indian Children have grown somewhat, say to the
> age of four or five, they have their hair cut for the first time.
> This is done superstitiously, inviting all the relatives, especially
> the *massas* and *cacas* (sons-in-law and maternal uncles). For
> the occasion, they fast and celebrate a festival to the *huaca* to
> whom they offer the young child. To the child they give wool,
> corn, sheep, silver and other things. On this occasion, his name
> is changed as noted above, as is that of the father and mother,
> to that of the *huaca* or *malquis*. The hair that is cut off they call
> *pacto* or *huaca* in the general language, *ñaca* in the lowlands and
> *pacto* in the sierra, and in some places, they make an offering

13. Bertonio, *Vocabulario,* p. 278 (translation mine).

of this hair or send it to the huaca or dangle it in front of it. In other places, the hair is kept in the house as a sacred object. We burned a quantity of this hair, or pact, in the towns we visited (italics are mine).[14]

After conducting a healing ceremony at Balsabe village, Marcelino asked me to be the *padrino* or godfather for his youngest son Martin to cut his first growth of hair. He brought the subject up again at his home a few days later. I accepted as I felt we were good friends and he had helped me a great deal in my research on local rites. The Sunday before the ceremony, Marcelino and his wife, Asunta, came to the parish house. Before asking for me, they consulted with the parish secretaries, Maria and Hipólito. Asunta told Maria that they wanted to have lunch but they did not want to eat alone. They had come to the house to see if I would accompany them but did not know if I would like their food. Maria assured them that I ate anything. With that, they called for me and asked me to eat with them. I invited them inside the parish house and shared some beer with their lunch of potatoes and *khespiño*, deep fried flat paddies of ground quinoa.

The following Saturday, I drove out to Marcelino's house with an ewe I had bought to give to Martin. The ewe was for the "hair for hair" trade in this rite. At Marcelino's request, I brought my tape player and some huayno tapes I had at home. We arrived at Marcelino's house about 3:00 p.m. We sat around for a while, listened to music and drank a beer. We had a lunch of khespiño, fried egg and *ch'uño*, freeze-dried potato. Marcelino then excused himself and left for a good while. When he returned, he had put on his best clothes. He asked for the coca I had brought and for an *incuña* for arranging and storing the cut hair. I had forgotten to bring confetti, so I made some by cutting some paper and candy wrappers with the scissors for the haircut. Marcelino, my new compadre, was very comfortable with me and commented, "My padrino can make anything but he cannot make children." That was the big joke of the evening given the confidence that Marcelino could joke about me.

The ritual is called an exchange of "hair for hair." Martin's hair would be traded for a sheep that would be his personal possession and the beginning of his wealth when the animal had offspring. As he cared for his sheep, he would be shepherding the family flock. This ceremony seemed to make five-year-old Martin into an adult with responsibilities. He and his peers skip childhood and start to work hard as shepherds out in the fields, in good and inclement weather. They have to answer for any lost sheep and face

---

14. Arriaga, *Extirpation*, p. 54.

a beating and no supper as a punishment. At this early age, they become responsible to protect the meager wealth of the family.

The ceremony was simple enough. Marcelino, Martin and I sat at the table where Asunta had set a plate with *quinoa* and another with *cañihuaco*, both grains native to the area. There was an empty plate with a coin on which to place the cut hair. The rest of the family stood in front of us. Adolfo, Martin's uncle, began the invocations and sprinkled some wine on all of us present.

Rotuchi ceremony, the first haircut of a 4–5-year-old child giving him/her family responsibilities and creating a deep bond between parent and sponsor.

Marcelino instructed us to pick up six coca leaves and offer them up with the quinoa and cañihua. We blew gently over the leaves and placed them on the empty plate. Marcelino put some confetti on my head and I on his. He put some on Martin's head. Marcelino said to me, "From now on I will call you *Padrino* and you will call me *compadre*. You will visit us always. This is our lucky day. Now we cut the hair." Asunta tied Martin's hair into small bunches so that we could each hold on to the part each was to cut. Once cut we put the tresses on the plate along with some money. I had not brought much money with me and gave very little. At some point, Asunta said, "Padrino cannot cut the hair evenly. Surely, the catechist did not teach him." Marcelino prayed for Martin that he be good and strong and live his life with a good heart. He prayed for all so that they would guide Martin in the good ways of life. I prayed also, invoking the Holy Spirit to guide me and the people closer to God.

After we finished cutting Martin's hair, Antonio, Marcelino's oldest son, brought in the ewe I was giving to Martin. Marcelino filled the scallop shells with wine and sprinkled both the sheep and the hair on the plate. At this point the ceremony ended.

Asunta served us some food with the beer I had brought. Afterwards, we played music and danced in that tiny room. We had a wonderful time, singing, dancing and drinking beer. The party ended about 9:00 p.m. and we all left for our respective homes.

This ritual made Marcelino and me *compadres*, literally co-parents. As compadres, Marcelino and I became more than brothers. I was no longer the distant observer, gleaning information to manipulate the people nor to destroy local native practices. My participation in this ceremony did not convert me to this native religion, but it confirmed Marcelino's trust in me. I trusted him, since he had taught me about the most intimate thoughts and ways of the people.

This mutual respect developed into a trust in people and resulted in very different welcome receptions at the villages I visited; it was unlike the way I was received when I went to celebrate Mass or to bless houses or visit the sick. My interest in and acceptance of the people with their beliefs and values opened them up to receive what I had to offer. It was not magic. I felt that if we could understand why the people stood against change, we might be able to alter gently the conditions for change toward a better life. I was in a position to be a bridge, that is a go-between for the missionaries and the Aymara people.

This effort to be with the Aymara in their rituals was very much in following the directives of the Second Vatican Council; I was working with other religions with respect and acceptance of the people. Ironically, it was CPE that turned my life around and made me see mission as listening to and hearing what people need.

4

Presenting the Aymara
Culture to the Outsider

*"Trust people as if they were what they ought to be
and you help them become what they are capable of becoming."*

—GOETHE[1]

THE AYMARA RITUALS I attended, recorded and analyzed did provide some answers as to why the Aymara adhered so tenaciously to their old ways and language. Although I perceived an adequate answer to my puzzlement about the Aymara's non-change, I was not sure where to go with what I had learned. Marcelino and the Aymara taught me so much about themselves that I felt confident to teach others about the religious mind of Andean peoples. I credit CPE training with my becoming more open and putting aside that natural reluctance to take other religions into consideration; that is, the attitude that my religion is the only true religion would have kept me at a distance from the Aymara as a superstitious people. Still, I had many questions resulting from this research and from my friendship with Marcelino. The first was how would I deal with the instruction from Jesus himself?

1. Goodreads.com/quotes.

"All power in heaven and on earth has been given to me. Go, therefore, and make disciples of all nations, baptizing them in the name of the Father, and of the Son, and of the Holy Spirit, teaching them to observe all that I have commanded you. And behold I am with you always, until the end of the age" (Matthew 28, 18–20).

The first Spanish missionaries followed this mandate from a different perspective; they came with a triumphant spirit stemming from Spain's defeat and expulsion of the Moors, as well as Jews, from Spain and utilized the court of the Inquisition to root out heretics. As a result of this outlook, they believed that they had to eradicate the religion of the newly conquered people. In contrast to what they had seen as diabolical and idolatrous practices, my observation was that the people were relating to God. Therefore, I attended the Aymara rites for two years, 1970 to 1972. At first, I was convinced that they were simply ignorant of an authentic religion. Like the missionaries before me, I was no match for the people's beliefs that were efficacious for them. As I looked at what the Aymara valued in their creeds and rites, I developed a different idea about religions. My thoughts on idolatry even changed, and, in my correspondence with my CPE supervisor, Bob Cholke, we believed that what was judged as idolatry was an attempt to reach the Almighty and that all religions we encounter are attempts to relate to God, a highly spiritual experience. Some religions have many gods and others have one God. Idolatry is not so much about the number of gods but the adoration of a god we have created, an artifact, the work of our hands. This is how Isaiah the prophet saw idolatry:

Idol makers all amount to nothing, and their precious works are of no avail, as they themselves give witness. . . He cuts down cedars. . . Half of it he burns in a fire and on its embers, he roasts his meat. . . Of what remains he makes a god, his idol, and prostrate before it in worship, he implores it, "Rescue me, for you are my god!" (Isaiah 44, 9–20)

In the prophet's eye, we adore our accomplishments and the material goods we have accumulated. Idolatry consists of having so much that we need no god since we have all we need. In a land where life is all work to put food on the table or to build a house from adobe bricks and straw, there is no accomplishment or artifact that becomes a people's god. The Aymara impressed me with the concept that, while they interact with the spirits, their hard work laid the basis for their religious attitudes. Alan Kolata, an author whom I read late in my writing, felt the same impact the Aymara had on me:

> Contrary to the received wisdom of observers unfamiliar with their resilience and resourcefulness, the Aymara are not passive victims of their environment. They shape the natural world around them with both their hands and their minds. . . On the high plateau, *spiritual insight flows from the hard living on the land*, from the yearly cycle of planting, irrigating, weeding, and harvesting. Ritual is grounded in reality, and reality becomes ritual. *Through their spiritual life, the Aymara seek health, abundance, and fertility, not a vague sense of harmony with Mother Earth*. . . Here the spiritual dimension is found in the ordinary acts and objects of everyday life: in the sound of water surging from a mountain's seam, in the smell of eucalyptus burning in the hearth, in the rich flavor of a new potato baked in the clay oven carved from the earth[2] (Italics mine).

People practice their ritual activity in order to communicate with God, with that totally Other, who is so awesome, and who makes their lives meaningful. The Aymara do have the *mullu,* which, they claim, is the spirit itself. They do not adore these figures, but they guard them with respect and pay homage to them by sprinkling them with wine and rubbing them with gold leaf (nowadays, with aluminum covered papers) two to four times a year. They are animistic, in that, any object, place, or phenomena possesses or contains a spirit with whom they interact.

During my study of local rites, I wrote several essays on the Aymara and their impact on our mission work within the Juli prelature, our mission area; there was no immediate response to these writings, but there were many questions about what I was doing. However, three events happened that supported my involvement with the Aymara rites, and clarified my giving predominant attention to these wonderful people. The first was with a visiting professor, Dr. Darryl Hobbs, who taught rural sociology at the University of Missouri in Columbia, Missouri; his wife and children accompanied him. He was a guest of Tony Macri, a fellow Maryknoller from a neighboring parish. After Tony showed Darryl what our mission entailed and the villages that we pastored, Darryl offered to conduct some basic classes for the missionaries about how to best work with rural groups. When I met Dr. Hobbs, I told him about my studying the local native rituals; and, although I was only eight months into the study, I had already written some essays interpreting what I saw and I wanted to continue studying as many different rites as possible. He asked me to present my findings to the mission personnel attending his classes to which I readily agreed.

---

2. Kolata, *Valley,* p.8.

The Monday prior to the presentation, Dr. Hobbs had asked me to explain how I, as a Catholic priest, could sit in on these sacrifices. He thought that I should be representing all that is against this sort of thing. Frankly, this question had not occurred to me since, initially, I was looking for evidence of natural sacraments, which are defined in theology as outward signs of the sacred and which confer some kind of grace on those who act on these signs.[3]

Dr. Hobbs raised many questions that I tried to cover in my lecture. He wondered how much the Aymara were willing to share with outsiders. Do they have a sense of boundary maintenance? Perhaps this did not apply to them. He asked if an Aymara is individualistic or driven by the group. What do the rites tell the participants? What was unique in the rites? What group concepts are present in the rites but not translatable? What about the concept of wealth, both individual and communal? What is prosperity? How is it defined and is it limited? What are their values and how do they express them in the rites? Do any modern artifacts appear in the ritual elements, like cars and radios? Finally, he asked if God knows men's minds when the Aymara perform these rites.

These were so many questions to answer in this presentation; the seminar began with a brief description of symbol and symbolic language. In the seminary, I studied this topic in depth because symbol connects us to the reality of beliefs and their effect on daily life. Symbols allow us to go beyond what we see in the tangible world of people of a different culture and to perceive their intangible world.

Presentation of Aymara Religious Rites

I described how I conducted my investigation, beginning at Sunday markets and talking to the sellers of the ritual elements, like the candy (*dulce misa*) or the metal figures (*chiuchi misa*), incense, llama fetuses and stone figures, called mullu. I showed the class the mullu or the talismans and the weavings used in rites, and explained their significance, their use and their connection to the local myths. I had acquired a considerable number of mullu stones; some purchased, but most were gifts from several *yatiri* and *pacco*. I showed pictures of the people involved in this sacred world. There were the merchants in the plaza who sell ritual items, the coca readers, and fortunetellers who can be seen in town and in the villages. As for the yatiri and pacco, there is at least one for every extended family. I took pictures of

---

3. Pope John Paul II, *Catechism*, p. 293.

the ceremonies I attended, and made recordings of conversations during those sessions.

We viewed pictures of three ceremonies that best illustrated the rites I attended. The first set of slides depicted the first plowing ceremony performed to combat wind, hail, and frost, as well as prayers for a good crop. This offering took place in full daylight at the field to be planted. The daytime pictures made it easy for the missionaries to follow each step of the planting rite. They saw that the villagers came together as a community with a single purpose and with a sense of security. With this ceremony, they wanted to protect their crops from nature's destructive elements. I pointed out the catechist in the picture as he was assigning places to the participants. The men sat with the officiating elders; the women sat together off to the side. The layout of the ceremonial elements is clearly visible.

A conventional layout of Aymara offering to Mother Earth, to the hill spirits and for healing. Included are coca leaves, llama fat, 2 bottles of wine or alcohol.

CATEDRAL - CUSCO

The Last Supper painting in the cathedral in Cuzco. Given the conventional
layout of a sacrificial offering, I am guessing that the Last Supper painting in
the cathedral in Cuzco, with the cuy (Guinea pig used in Inca sacrifices) conveys
the notion of sacrifice. The painting may have been used to teach the sacrificial
character of the Last Supper.

The whole ceremony included all present to take part; one by one,
everyone prayed with their coca leaves and added them to their sacrificial
offering. After everyone had prayed and made their invocations, the sacrificial elements were bundled in a large sheet of paper, along with llama fat
and incense; then, the officiating yatiri wrapped the offering in an incuña
and brushed all the participants with this bundle, because this offering
came from every member of this community. Afterwards, he burned the
sacrifice at the rim of an ancient grave called a *gentile*, a word probably
borrowed from the missionaries' vocabulary to describe non-believers or
heathens. The traditional name given to this grave is *huaca*, a sacred stone.

The village leaders burn the communal offering at the base of the village huaca.

All villages have one or more huacas as their protective spirits. The service ended with all the villagers having lunch together.

Another ceremony of the whole community was the *apóostol misa,* so called for the twelve children selected to be the twelve apostles, namely, the principal spirits of this village. This rite takes place at night after a lightning strike as an effort to dispel the death threats that Santiago, the hurler of thunderbolts, had brought upon this village. The remarkable part of this ritual was the pacco's lifting up of an owl on a cross to ward off death from this lightning strike. The ceremony ends at sunrise as the community now faces a new dawn and a new life.

Finally, we looked at the *salud misa* or the table for good health, the rite that is most common for healing and for the yearly offering to Mother Earth. The details of these rites and beliefs gave the missionaries a picture of how the Aymara see themselves.

The visual showcase ended with an analysis of who the Aymara are based on their religious practices; for them, this religion creates a balance in life by adhering to the traditional ways, and targets the family as strongly united and supportive. They have a strong sense of group and these rites strengthen this social bond since a whole village heals and recovers strength with the salud misa for an individual. The balance coming from this ritual action allows a person to make transitions in life in the company of others. The Aymara find both meaning and a moral code in their religion; they handle individual deviancy through the rules of conduct that emerge from the ritual, a moral code that reflects the Aymara way of life and allows an offender to live within this community.

Two other values are the well-being of animals and the protection of crops from the elements, as these are the basis for their economic security. The forces of nature, they believe, are spirits that destroy their crops and the economy of the Aymara. As they consult the spirits in the salud misa, they receive promises of a good crop. The power of the pacco amazed me as he made recommendations or foretold the birth of a new child. While anthropologists have seen the Aymara as fatalistic and submissive, they failed to recognize that the Aymara suffer from racial discrimination and cannot enter the mainstream society as equals. They have good reasons to follow the recommendations from the pacco or yatiri because they make sense to them. This is a down-to-earth spirituality detected in the culture and lifestyle of the Aymara.

My missionary colleagues and I need to take these expressions seriously in order to understand how the people think and feel about family, community and their lives. They tend to their spiritual needs naturally. My photos and transcripts of the ceremonies demonstrated their values and the direction of their lives.

Dr. Hobbs commented that the presentation was devastating because the data presented made the men ask themselves about the value of their work. They had spent as much as fifteen to twenty years in this mission. It appeared that only now they were getting to know the reality of this region. The men were visibly stunned at the thought that their efforts appeared fruitless since they did not know the local religious world. I had noticed that several men had copies of Tchopik's study on the Aymara that included detailed accounts of the Aymara rites. Fr. John Schiff had also printed up a brief description of their various beliefs and practices. The information I presented could not have been that new, but this report did have a shocking effect. Perhaps it was the depth with which I had studied these rites that opened their eyes to the Aymara world. Some priests felt that I was giving a native religion the same status as our Catholic religion. Others said I was making all religions the same and that this was an error on my part. This was not the case at all for I recognized a profound and authentic spirituality in the Aymara religion.

Dr. Hobbs had further suggestions on applying and utilizing this newly revealed information; namely, that we put this information into an organizational context. If we say we need more information and go on looking, we are making an excuse for not doing anything. He stated that evaluations should lead to modification, not to a justification for our presence in this area. Furthermore, the poorer the quality of organization, the lower would be the probability for change. An example is in the difficulty for a man to be ordained in the church. The institution responds, "It was hard for me. It should be hard for you."

This is not an answer coming out of good organization. Dr. Hobbs made these recommendations after the exposition of the rites. His suggestion to present this material to the missionaries was a Godsend because it helped us focus more professionally on our ministry.

This talk encouraged several priests to introduce the use of incense into the Masses in the manner the Aymara offer it in their rites. They also incorporated the pardon gestures from the Aymara rites so that the Mass would produce its intended effect. The people responded positively to these changes, but it did not become the practice in all parishes. Still the missionaries' response gave credence and acceptance to my studying the native religion.

Some early chroniclers found the native moral precepts so impressive that they interpreted local myths of Thunupa as depicting visits by St. Thomas, the apostle, or St. Bartholomew or even by Jesus Christ. In spite of these musings, it is difficult to say that the contemporary Aymara define themselves as Christian. Our task as missionaries is to include in their beliefs the presence of Christ as Lord and as Savior, not as a magical element in their rites. In my transcripts, no shaman mentioned Christ in their rites, except in making the sign of the cross with "*dios auki, dios yoka, dios espiritu santo*" (God Father, God Son, God Holy Spirit). However, the Christian influence of the past 400 years has given the Aymara religion a broader vocabulary and some added ritual actions. If the Aymara do not see themselves as Christian, what, then, is the Aymara if not Christian? We simply need to look for what is meaningful to an Aymara. The people in town also have these rites performed for their crops. The degree of education or sophistication did not seem to make a difference when it came to the ritual expression of the people's values.

What would things be like if the pacco or the spirits recommended fertilizers, vaccinations, house-sweeping, cash crops, stoves lifted off the floor, or new foodstuffs that can grow in high altitudes?

The pacco always invokes the hill spirits in all of the ceremonies and that practice made the hills around Ilave very alive to me. The people identify them as *achachilanaca*, as ancestors or grandfathers, consult them, and make offerings to placate them. The hills are the projections of what the people expect of themselves and give life to their ideals, hopes and well-being. The hills are the images of the Aymara, a people of the Altiplano as solid, permanent and high above everything else. These symbols bring to mind the words of the Psalmist who says:

> I raise my eyes toward the mountains
> From where will my help come?
> My help comes from the Lord,
> The maker of heaven and earth.
> God will not allow your foot to slip;
> Your guardian does not sleep. . .
> The Lord will guard you from all evil,
> Will always guard your life.
> The Lord will guard your coming and your going
> Both now and forever. (Psalm 121, 1–3 and 7–8)

At the same time, they are aware of the contemporary world of schooling, the money economy, and methods to improve farming and animal husbandry. Once, in a ceremony, Marcelino asked what time it was and a young man said, "It is 11:45." I looked at my watch and he was correct. He added that a plane flies over this area every night at 11:45 p.m. There are many other examples of their awareness of life outside of the Aymara environment.

Filming the documentary "The Healer"

The second incident that brought attention to missionaries' working with the yatiri and the pacco was Maryknoll's decision to produce a film documentary as part of a larger Maryknoll project on the theme of *concientización* (originally *conscientização*).[4] Maryknoll wanted to show how missionary priests develop this social conscience among their parishioners. The concept of concientización came from Paulo Freire's book *Pedagogy of the Oppressed*. Paulo Freire, a Brazilian educator, promoted a method of education by which the oppressed could free themselves from oppression and then proceed to free the oppressors from subjugating others. The sites for filming were Guatemala, Chile, and Peru.

The film, produced in Peru in December of 1972, two years after beginning the study of the rites, turned out to be the opposite of *concientización*. It was more about how the people whom I pastored had influenced and changed me, the missionary. Maryknoll informed me of the project but did not have a date for filming. Meanwhile, in November of 1972, I was taking part in a workshop at the Maryknoll novitiate in Massachusetts. As we were

---

4. Freire, *Pedagogy*, pp. 17–19.

finishing up, I got word to hurry back to Peru because the film crew was to arrive in Puno the first week of December. I made a quick visit with my parents and left for Peru. Both the film crew and I arrived in Puno on the same day and we were to drive out to Ilave that evening. Since we were in a hurry, we left without eating. Halfway to Ilave, we lost a wheel of our Jeep. We were stuck into the night on a lonely road; it was raining hard that night and there was no traffic on the road. Finally, a truck came by and we sent a message to Ilave that we had broken down on the road, still some twenty miles from Ilave. Puno was about thirty-six miles from Ilave.

We were getting hungry in that jeep, loaded with baggage and filming equipment. The crew consisted of Tom Cohen, Bill Christianson, and Richard Pierce, the camera operator. Now one thing that I had missed in Peru was cheese. I did not miss running water, all day electricity and other amenities of city life. However, I did miss cheese. I had brought some small wedges of bleu cheese with me when I left the States. Although I treasured this cheese, we had to eat it all up for lack of supper. We ate the cheese with the wine used for Mass, as there was no other foodstuff in the car.

When we arrived in Ilave, we started planning what we were going to film. When I first heard of the projected documentary, I planned to call the local healers and diviners together to have a mini convention of these wise men since we could discuss the local beliefs and expectations of the people in this region. However, we decided to go see Marcelino, who had been my principal informant, to ask for his input.

The next morning, when we arrived at Marcelino's house, we found out that Marcelino's youngest son, Martincito, had died that night. The news crushed me because this boy was so loveable, and I was godfather for his rotuchi, his first haircut.

Tom Cohen said that we could film the funeral. I felt badly that we were imposing on Marcelino at this difficult time; nonetheless, I asked Marcelino if this would be acceptable to him, and I explained what filming these moments involved. I told him that these visitors would be up close with cameras and would be giving instructions to each other. Marcelino was comfortable with this arrangement.

I had bought a new pair of shoes for Martincito. He was never able to wear them but I gave them to Marcelino anyway. We returned to the parish to pick up the cameras. When we returned to Marcelino's village, the family and neighbors were already constructing the tiny coffin out of discarded wooden crates. Marcelino and his wife, Asunta, were preparing the body for burial. Finally, Marcelino came out with Martincito's body wrapped in a blanket. He, then, put the boy's body in the small coffin. The custom there is that the closest relative of the deceased places the body in the coffin. Thus, when a man dies, the wife puts his body in the coffin or vice versa, with the man putting his wife's body in the coffin. Martincito's brother and sister put in some of their brother's toys with his body. Among them was a little plastic Volkswagen, Martincito's favorite toy. He loved it because I drove a Volkswagen and Martincito always told his parents that he was going to be like his godfather. When his parents argued or yelled at each other, this little boy would tell them that he was going to run away, join his godfather, and stay with me.

The crew was documenting a very painful moment and to this day, I still feel a lump in my throat when I see this movie. I loved this family deeply. Martincito's body was buried about two hundred meters uphill from his house, since there are no cemeteries in these villages.

The movie also followed conversations I had with Marcelino about his son. Marcelino said his son's death would give the family some kind of reward from the spirits. Deaths of children appear to be a payment or a sacrifice to the major spirits of the area; the spirits, in turn, will give the people better crops or stronger animals. This belief eases the pain of losing one's child who is now an angel who watches over the family.

We also filmed a prayer meeting in one of the villages; there, I brought up the topic of the death of my godson and the death of any child. I had picked as a reading the text from 2 Samuel chapter 13, verses 13—18, in which David was being punished for his sin. God forgave David but was to take the life of his son. David fasted and prayed for his son's life but the son died anyway. The discussion covered whether the death of a child was a punishment or a payment to the spirits. People here see so many misfortunes as punishment from the spirits, especially disasters regarding crops and raising animals. However, they do not attribute a death as a punishment but as something owed to the spirits. We also asked where the souls of the dead go. The discussion was lengthy and brought out the beliefs of the people. They were frank in sharing their opinions and beliefs, especially about the afterlife as heaven for some and a big unknown for the majority.

Finally, we filmed a salud misa, the healing ritual, which best depicts both the ritual actions and the beliefs of the people. Two young women, Benita and Eduarda, were ill and the family had asked Marcelino to conduct this healing ceremony for them. At this time, we decided to call the film, "The Healer." Other scenes in the movie were of the villages of Jach'a Winchoca, Marcelino's home, and Jamach'occo, as well as in the town of Juli, and some farming areas surrounding the town of Ilave.

The film closes with my stating that my role is to discover God in the people, in their customs, and in the hill spirits. This documentary invites the audience to go into what is profound in the minds and spiritual lives of people. Augustine does this in the *Confessions*: ". . .I entered even into my inward self, Thou, being my guide. . .And I entered and beheld with the eye of my soul. . .the Light Unchangeable (God)."[5] The movie does not convey information but rather the experience of the powerful presence of God.

The documentary had an impressive acceptance within Maryknoll, Catholic reflection groups, and even some anthropology classes in various universities. The film appeared in other countries with the respective language dubbed in. In the United States, ABC television ran a nationwide showing of the film, "The Healer", as part of their series, Directions, thanks to the efforts of Fr. Don Casey, director of Maryknoll's World Horizon Films; the program included an interview with Fr. Raymond Hill, then superior general of Maryknoll.[6] The discussion focused on Maryknoll's missionary efforts as seen in the documentary.

The success of the movie gave me the opportunity to speak both in Peru and in the United States about getting to know indigenous peoples and seeing them as our equals. Fr. Jim Madden best described this experience when a yatiri went up to him, put his arm around Jim and said, "You and I are equal" because he felt and expressed what Jim Madden had been practicing while he was living in an Aymara village. We are their equals; they are our equals. I saw that my work targeted first recognizing and accepting indigenous groups, then, once comfortable in their company, direct evangelizing of them.

In contrast, my colleagues in Ilave and Puno exhibited indifference during the filming. Several kept reminding me not to let this filming go to my head. I simply continued working in my usual fashion with local communities. When I got a copy of the film, so many people borrowed it that I lost track of who had the film and never got it back. Many years later, I received a pale copy on a VHS tape.[7]

After the release of the film, two other groups came to Ilave to film our work with the Aymara. One was from a Dutch TV station and the other from a German company. These were documentaries with no compensation for the people filmed in the process. It did not occur to me to ask for something for these communities. Later, a university student from Juli showed me an op-ed article in a Mexican magazine, stating that "The Healer" described the kind of missionaries the people needed. These later incidents all taught an even broader audience about the closeness of indigenous groups to us, a lesson the Maryknoll Missionary Society has spread through its mission work.

5. Augustine, *The Confessions*, p. 1.

6. Funke, "How One Priest, 29.

7. "The Healer" is available at: https://www.worldcat.org/title/healer/oclc/15643183.

Catechist Training Based on Aymara Beliefs

The third incident that supported my involvement with a different religion was using local beliefs to develop leadership skills among the catechists. In this instance, my teaching material was the local belief in the loss of one's soul. Generally, the Aymara claim that a person becomes ill because he or she has lost his/ her soul. For most yatiri, the most requested rite is that of calling back a lost soul. The Aymara describe this lost condition with expressions like "*animojj chhakatawa*," "*janiu animunkiti*," and "*animupajj usutawa.*" These phrases can be translated as, "he/she has lost his/her spirit," "he has no spirit left," and "he/she is sick to his/her soul." For the Aymara, a person has three souls: the baby soul, the w*awa*, then, the shadow or the *qamasa* and finally the adult soul, the *ajayu*. The baby soul is lost (*qenqo* or *catjja*) by a simple jarring, or by a frightening experience like exploding fireworks or large crowds of strangers. The second soul, qamasa, is lost due to a deeply traumatic experience creating a mental breakdown. The third soul, ajayu, is lost when a person dies and is buried in the grave with the deceased person. I observed several of the salud misa in which Marcelino called the baby soul back to the ill person.

This belief reminded me of Carl Jung, whose works I had read extensively for research for a paper on symbol; he experienced the loss of his soul, which he describes in his book, *Memories, Dreams, and Reflections*:

> I have written down a fantasy of my soul having flown away from me. This was a significant event. The soul, the anima, established the relationship to the unconscious. In a certain sense, this is also a relationship to the collectivity of the dead, the land of the ancestors. If, therefore, one has a fantasy of the soul vanishing, this means that it has withdrawn into the unconscious, or into the land of the dead. There it produces a mysterious animation and gives visible form to the ancestral traces, to the collective content. Like a medium, it gives the dead a chance to manifest themselves. Therefore, soon after the disappearance of my soul, the 'dead' appeared to me and the result was the 'Septem Sermones' (a separate work called Seven Sermons to the Dead).[8]

Jung hit at the core of loss of soul as a universal experience; what he observed is contained in the following descriptions that people have given me. I did not impose Jung's narrative on Aymara stories but recognized his perceptions in the accounts told to me. When a child or an adult loses his or her baby soul, that person becomes sick, refuses to eat, stops eating, or

8. Jung, *Memories*, pp. 191 and 378.

vomits, and becomes listless. For Jung, this soul has gone to the land of the dead and has to be called back to life. Sometimes, for the Aymara, this loss of soul occurs when a malicious or ambivalent spirit takes hold of the wawa soul. A number of people from this area have described these spirits as mermaids in water holes or springs, or as galloping horsemen in crevices on the side of a hill. After the Spanish introduced the horse to this region, the people came to believe that evil spirits, now the foreigner, ride on horseback to steal the whole person, body and soul.

I recall that as a child in Texas during the early 1940's, pilots in training for air combat used to buzz our Mexican-American community in their fighter planes. We could see the pilots clearly laughing at us from their cockpits. My grandmother would run us into the house, herding us like scared sheep. Once inside, she covered our heads with a towel or a blanket. This was not protection! In a way, she was trying to keep our souls inside of us. She was keeping our souls intact. My grandmother was a natural healer who believed that the evil spirits in the noise of the fighter planes could have made us sick or, as I look back, "taken our souls."

The yatiri or pacco invokes the spirits to inquire which one took the soul; then, through a ritual payment to that spirit, the yatiri can call the soul back into a sick person and the patient snaps out of the ailment and regains his/her soul. From a stage of listlessness, of not eating, of high fever, and being bedridden, the person regains his/her soul and is healthy again. A child eats again and can sleep well at night. An adult goes out to the patio and gathers some barley or gets the animals ready for pasture. The neighbors see this person as well and the village becomes complete again. Healing is for a whole community. In his writings, Arriaga prohibited new Christians from performing this salud misa because it would strengthen their belief in the healing power of this religion.[9]

When a person loses his second soul or the qamasa, this becomes more difficult to heal because a greater part of a person has gone to the land of the dead. Since evil places have a stronger hold of the *qamasa*, the person passes out or dies. A young woman, Feliciana, told me that her mother had died three times. When she regained consciousness, the family told her how they had tried to revive her by grabbing her and pulling her hair. The family had been crying because the woman had really died. Nevertheless, she finally woke up and recounted her dreams. She said that her neighbor who had died recently had come to get her and together they had climbed a ladder that led to the upper corner of the room. She then went onto the roof of the

9 Arriaga, *The Extirpation*, p.99.

house and kept climbing up the ladder until they came to a river. The dead neighbor left her there telling her to cross the river.

After crossing the river, she continued walking until she came to a town square, in which everything was silver. There she saw her father who had died the year before. He greeted her and asked her where her husband and her children were. He asked, "Why are you acting lazy like this? Why don't you work?" Then he took her around the plaza admiring the beauty of the silver streets. She called this walking through heaven. Having walked about quite a bit she was tired and sat down to rest. Her father told her she was lazy and she should return to her husband and children. Therefore, she went back, descended the ladder and climbed into her bed. She awoke perfectly well and was so happy that she talked about this dream for a number of years.

Feliciana's story, however, was exceptional. Ordinarily, the shamans are afraid of healing a person who has lost the qamasa. They find that the person is far too sick, and experience has taught them that at the moment of regaining the shadow soul, the person dies. This was the case of a woman, Yolanda, whom I had visited to administer the sacrament of the sick. Visiting her was when I learned that people here believe that the soul wanders about just before dying. When I got to the house, I nearly collided with Yolanda's aunt, who came running out of the house visibly frightened, perspiring and out of breath, because she had had a terrifying experience. She told me that she had been going to Yolanda's house and saw her walking in a hurry; as she approached her, Yolanda walked rapidly by her and seemed to be in a hurry. Her aunt tried to catch up with her and called her, but Yolanda did not answer. Since the aunt tired easily, she stopped for a while. Up ahead she saw Yolanda reaching some other people and passing them. This scene alarmed the aunt, and she hurried to Yolanda's house to see if she had died or was dying because people believe that the soul appears to people in this fleeting and hurried fashion before dying.

I went in to see Yolanda. She was in bed and looked perfectly well to me. I told her so, and I asked why she had sent for me; she said she was going to die and wanted the sacrament of the holy oils before she died. I talked with her for a little while about being well and not needing the sacrament, but she insisted on receiving the holy oils. Then I proceeded to talk to her about meeting with God and going into the presence of God forever. We prayed for a while and I anointed her with the holy oils. Yolanda died that evening. The Aymara believe that Yolanda's soul revealed itself because she was near death; she had lost her soul and was going to the land of the dead.

It seems that people have a two-dimensional view of the past, like looking at a photograph. Everything seems to be on that flat view with no dimension of the past or the present. This two-dimensional view of the past is a way of expressing those ancestral places and traces of the collective memories as a here-and-now reality. The language used in the rites is both past and present. It is ancestral in the sense that they talk to the achachila and to all the place spirits that have been there from the age of darkness. This is what I have seen when the achachila tells the people present to consult with the maestro, the yatiri. The yatiri has the best advice for them at that moment. The hero, then, is the achachila, who is not a type of god but the present hero. This confirms what Jung says; namely, that when the soul vanishes into the unconscious, it produces a visible form of the ancestral traces of the collective content.[10]

The Aymara live in constant fear of punishment for offending these unseen spirits. For Jung, these ancestral places are the unconscious or they are a conglomeration of all the memories of childhood, which connect with the memories of their parents and their grandparents and so on for generations, for centuries. These traditions remain in folk lore as both fear-causing as well as life-giving rites, which are collective; they are preserved and observed for their revitalizing value.

Accompanying this belief of loss of soul is the manner in which people deal with death. From my observations, the Aymara accept it as if handling a cup or a plate. It seems tangible because the soul that goes into the land of the dead returns to talk about what he/she has seen there. Our sacristan always accompanied me when I went to visit the sick. After I had attended several rites, he informed me that when a priest visits the sick to administer the holy oils, if he looks up and to the right when he exits the house, the person would regain his health. If the priest looks down as he leaves, the person will die. I tried making it a point to look up and to the right, but no one regained good health. Apparently, this practice was hearsay, as it did not work for me; the other missionaries were not aware of this belief.

In this particular belief of loss of soul, people express what they need to be free, to be saved. The real world of the Aymara contains much of what is in the belief of the three souls. What the three souls really indicate, to my mind, is the threefold breakdown of the Aymara's sense of history, his conscious and unconscious personality. Perhaps this is really a question of mental illness, or it is simply a withdrawing into the unconscious when the soul vanishes. This may be how an Aymara describes mental illness, and at the same time, he or she recognizes a prophet, who tells of his having visited the land of the dead, of the ancestors. The pastor in the town of Yunguyo told me of his experience of "Mamata", a woman who seemed completely crazy and out of touch with reality, yet she was highly respected because

10. Jung, *Dreams*, p. 191.

people said she was prophesizing and they followed closely what she said. This is an example of how to understand the Aymara when they speak of the loss of soul and regaining it.

It occurred to me to integrate this belief into a mature, fear-free setting that people could understand. I had read *I'm OK—You're OK, Games People Play*[11] and other material on Transactional Analysis. I thought that the three souls fit into this model of parent, child and adult in which the parent's vocabulary is *always* or *never*, constantly demanding or judging; the child's response is happy and outgoing or scared and withdrawn. The adult takes the parent and child responses to correct or validate them in order to let a person live as freely and humanly as possible. I decided to try applying this model in some training sessions with the catechists. Jung inspired me to present this training when he stated in his book, *Man and His Symbols*, that belief in several souls "means that the individual psyche is far from being safely synthesized; on the contrary, it threatens to fragment only too easily under the onslaught of unchecked emotions."[12]

I began the training by talking to the catechists about the three souls; there was an immediate connection because they knew this belief. By applying the TA model to the three souls, I tried to get the catechists to understand what is going on when they deal with others, especially the people who criticize or reject their work or their role in the church. What people say or how they respond contain the clues that alert the catechists whether they are dealing with a parent, a child or an adult. The names I used to describe these aspects of a person were the parent as the qamasa (el *amo,* the master, the hacienda owner, the critic or other similar roles). The child is the wawa (the baby, playful, moody, sad, crying or cheerful, the creative, full-of-wonder type). The adult I called the ajayu, the person, the decision maker. As we role played different situations, I asked who was in charge at that moment. They responded clearly and understood the roles of each of the three souls in this fashion.

My goal in this training was to have the catechists act more independently and more maturely than mere translators and to teach more than catechism. I wanted them to think of what they were teaching and to reason beyond the catechism material they taught villagers. I wanted them to know who they are, what drives them and where they are going. This was especially urgent as the catechists were exercising so many new charges, like that of being a lay pastor of the villages, where they served and presided at prayer services instead of a priest celebrating a fiesta Mass. Our bishop, Edward

11. Harris, *I'm OK.*

12. Jung, *Man,* p. 8.

Fedders, had requested of Rome to have these new pastors ordained, but he was denied; they remained laymen with ministerial charges and were, in effect, replacing the priests.[13]

I wanted them to teach the people how to feel in control of their lives. The belief system had taught the people to fear forces of nature as beings with whom one could negotiate and convince them not to punish the people. This is a cultural tradition that, if ignored, the people would pay the consequences. This traditional kind of thinking does not leave much room for determining one's outcome in life, since fear of these invisible beings dominates people's lives. The local belief of the three souls helped them regain control and to feel a sense of personal power. I did not criticize or go after the achachila or the yatiri, but found power in them to teach the people to be responsible for each other, while the catechists were to carry on the Christian message of love and justice with this new sense of responsibility and a new sense of life.

Since evangelization aims at change rather than destruction, this approach with the catechists made use of an accepted, readily understood Aymara worldview. Now, this same belief served as the basis for change in which the catechists grasped the kind of self-direction that would give people the freedom of choosing how to live their lives, not out of fear but out of the inner power of faith. We worked toward a faith experience the catechists can share with the communities where they lived. This training marked that change.

It worked. The catechists thought it was the best thing they had learned to date. If I had not studied the local rites and beliefs, I would never have tried applying something I knew from my background as fitting into the local way of thinking. Here was a bridge between two cultures; and I felt I was a bridge between the Aymara and the missionary personnel. The success in relying on the belief of the three souls in a training setting was not taking advantage of the Aymara because we managed to know their culture and beliefs; rather it was based on a mutual, intercultural path of growth for the Aymara, for missionaries and for the public that viewed "The Healer". Our ministry was growing as the result of our having entered into a dialogue with a religion different from Catholicism. We were no longer fighting a war to extirpate idolatry.

These three events marked notable changes beginning with our mission personnel; their becoming familiar with the religion of the Aymara created opportunities for change in our pastoral work. Next, the documentary, "The Healer", presented a new view of mission that went beyond Mass

---

13. Fitzpatrick-Behrens, *The Maryknoll*, p. 276, note 27.

and baptisms to the spiritual needs of the people and their solution to such needs. Finally, relying on traditional Aymara beliefs to retrain the catechists changed the routine patterns of their work to a more creative way of instructing their communities. For me, these three incidents directed me to provide a different kind of teaching, an awakening of the people. These three events opened the door to greater change.

5

A Sense of Dignity

The Aymara Find Self-Worth

"You cannot uneducate (sic) the person who has learned to read. You cannot humiliate the person who feels pride. You cannot oppress the people who are not afraid anymore."

—Cesar Chavez[1]

"Start by doing what's necessary; then do what's possible; and suddenly you are doing the impossible."

—St. Francis of Assisi

My using the belief of the three souls as part of training the catechists with their enthusiastic response, as well as the impact of Aymara spirituality on the missionary personnel, encouraged me to inquire what else we could do based on local culture and beliefs. My own appreciation and love for the Aymara moved me strongly to find a way of bettering their lives, to have them seen and heard; however, change and growth would have to come from the values that have guided the people throughout the centuries of their existence. My primary interest focused on finding a way by which

1. Chavez, Goodreads

the Aymara could take a stand in contemporary society on the strength of
their history.

Given their lowly position in the social structure, they reminded me
of the *anawim*, the poor of God, as found in Isaiah 61:1 and repeated in
Luke 4, 18–19:

> The Spirit of the Lord Yahweh is upon me, because Yahweh has
> anointed me to bring good news to the anawim: He has sent me
> to bind up the brokenhearted, to proclaim liberty to captives
> and freedom to prisoners.

We decided to organize reflection-action groups as disclosed in Paulo
Freire's *Pedagogy of the Oppressed* and Gustavo Gutierrez's *A Theology for
Liberation*, "The spirituality of liberation will have as its basis the spirituality
of the *anawim*."[2]

Paulo Freire was born in Recife, in northeast Brazil where in his youth
he experienced the widespread poverty of the Depression. He decided early
that he wanted to work with the poor, became an educator and worked with
illiterate adults and became famous for teaching adults to read and write in
a forty-five-day course. He developed a critical pedagogy based on observe,
reflect and act, as the process of overcoming a state of oppression and alien-
ation of the poor.

> Human activity consists of action and reflection; it is transfor-
> mation of the world. . . .it requires theory to illuminate it. Hu-
> man activity is theory and practice; it is reflection and action.[3]

This process comes about by going beyond knowing one's condition
but acting as a group to transform one's reality; this is the praxis of life,
conscientizeção, namely, "learning to perceive social, political and economic contradictions, and to take action against the oppressive elements of
reality."[4] Freire saw the people as the subjects "who meet to name the world
in order to transform it"[5] and "history is not waiting for my death in order
to say, that man existed."[6] I was fascinated with the notion that each of us
makes history. "The future of history belongs to the poor and exploited."[7]
Our mission work, then, must be our participation in the creation and the
development of history.

2. Gutierrez, p.120.

3. Freire, *Pedagogy,* p. 106.

4. Freire, *Pedagogy,* note 1, p. 17.

5 Freire, p.148.

6. Freire, tx.cpusa.org.

7. Gutierrez, *A Theology,* p.120.

Gutierrez, a Dominican priest, wrote his book, *A Theology of Liberation*, from reflecting on his pastoral experiences while working with the poor. He pointed out how his pastoral encounters provoked reflection on the word of God in the face of abject poverty and the oppression of the poor. For him, poverty is a situation that destroys peoples, families and individuals. Fate does not create poverty but appears from the actions of those in power.[8] When Gutierrez presented his theology to the Latin American bishops' conferences (CELAM) in Medellin, Colombia, and in Puebla, Mexico, the bishops adopted his work and defined poverty as "institutionalized violence."[9] Furthermore, they accepted this theology and adopted as pastoral practice the "preferential option for the poor."[10] Dr. Paul Farmer, a later follower of Gutierrez, pointed out how people miss seeing the mistreatment of the poor because this violence does not "involve bullets, knives or instruments of torture; this misery has often eluded those seeking to identify violence and its victims."[11] This theology begins from the ground up with the poor and affects the whole church in an effort to think clearly about the meaning of religious faith in the context of oppression, poverty, and inequality. This pursuit demanded the effort on our part as pastors to be compassionate and courageous and respond with life-sustaining efforts to change those conditions. It is a practical theology in the language of the people. It creates and supports the efforts to pursue justice and helps people to sense the incongruity between celebration of the Eucharist and exploitation from injustice. This approach gives theology of liberation a militant air because it looks for change, for justice. As Gutierrez points out:

> This gives rise to a serious confrontation between Christians who suffer injustice and exploitation and those who benefit from the established order. Under such circumstances, life in the contemporary Christian community becomes particularly difficult and conflictual. Participation in the Eucharist, for example, as it is celebrated today, appears too many to be an action, which, for want of the support of an authentic community, appears an exercise in make-believe.[12]

Liberation theology is a perfect parallel to Freire's education for liberation from the oppressors' preventing subjugated people "from being fully human" and referring to them as "those people . . . the envious masses . . .

8. Gutiérrez, p. 166.
9. Gutiérrez., p. xxi.
10. Gutiérrez, *A Theology*, p. xxv.
11. Farmer, *Pathologies*, p.8.
12. Gutierrez, *A Theology*, p. 75.

savages . . . subversives."[13] Once free, the subjugated can educate the oppressor from the conviction of having to exploit others. We did not set out to study Freire or Gutierrez and their ideology, but the environment in which we worked demanded that we work along with this theology/ideology.

The pastoral practice that Gutierrez recommends is, primarily, collaboration among the faithful through *comunidades eclesiales de base,* namely, base-level ecclesial communities. These are grass roots Christian groups whose members reflect and assess, in union with their pastors, their own lives, their faith and their place in history, that is, people place their experiences, no matter how small, into a given point in history. This sharing takes them out of their limitations, ready to change their world. They restore their dignity, as is the purpose of the theology for liberation.

Since such claims encroach on the comfort zone of the powerful and wealthy, these authoritarian types question the legitimacy of these groups' power to change things. These objections bring people's attention to the poor who have been the invisible and voiceless and who now begin to have a place in history. Gutierrez finds support and clarification in the Vatican II Pastoral Constitution, *Gaudium et Spes,* on the participation and full recognition of the poor:

> The joys and the hopes, the grief and the anxieties of the men
> of this age, especially those who are poor or in any way afflicted
> these are the joys and hopes, the grief and anxieties of the fol-
> lowers of Christ. Indeed, nothing genuinely human fails to raise
> an echo in their hearts. For theirs is a community composed of
> men. United in Christ, they are led by the Holy Spirit in their
> journey to the Kingdom of their Father and they have welcomed
> the news of salvation, which is meant for every man. That is why
> this community realizes that it is truly linked with mankind and
> its history by the deepest of bonds.[14]

I wanted the Aymara to stand up, to speak up and to be heard, something like the creatures in the speck of dust in Dr. Seuss's whimsical story *Horton Hears the Who.* We now knew what we had to do: we needed to let the people be in charge of their own life goals. Therefore, forming reflection-action groups was not a whim or a search for something to do; Paulo Freire and Gustavo Gutierrez had clarified our task and we were ready.

Preparation for this kind of direction began with the choice of villages to visit. First, I had looked at ongoing projects around me; these included Maryknoll's indigenous apostolate, the leadership programs at the Rural

13. Freire, *Pedagogy,* p.38.
14. Gutierrez, *A Theology,* p. 75.

Institute in Juli and the ongoing catechist training programs which gave me a sense of direction. Furthermore, I recalled advice that Dr. Hobbs had given us in his mini-class on rural sociology, namely, that communities an hour from the center are the ones most likely to develop. When villagers came into town, I would ask them how long it took them to travel into town. If their villages were an hour away, they were the ones we chose to begin this new education. After having chosen the communities where we would work, I took the next step.

First, I took pictures of the people in the chosen villages in their everyday activities like farming, cooking, building houses, just everyday activities. As I took the photographs, I assured the residents that I would return to show them the pictures. Next, we calculated that a series of nine meetings over a period of nine weeks would be sufficient time for people to look at themselves and assess where they were. When life for an Aymara is routine, there is no sense of finding one's place in history, worse yet, not making history.

Planning the structure and content of the meetings did not involve the other priests of the parish, primarily, because I was alone in the parish for several days at a time. Moreover, the other priests had other interests and activities; therefore, I worked closely with Domingo, the sacristan, with Hipólito, the office secretary, and Trinidad, our cook. They liked the concept behind the meetings, especially, conducting them between 6:00 and 7:00 in the evening on a weekly basis for nine weeks; the time was ideal for the communities. Domingo and Hipólito were already used to my night activities, as they had accompanied me regularly when I attended the local all-night rituals. From these rituals, the villagers were already disposed to meeting at night, when people were at home and not busy with the potato fields or pasturing animals. Domingo and Hipólito appreciated the fact that we were going to put the results of those visits into something useful for the people and for the Church.

We began! We started our first group in June, 1972 in Anccasaya, three miles outside of town, where we met at the community center, a 20 by 25-foot adobe room with a thatch roof. The nice thing about a thatch roof is that when it rains the sound is soft, soothing like a mother's hand, patting down the child's blanket as he falls asleep. A smooth coat of mud covered the adobe seams and gave it a more finished look. Since there were no tables, chairs, or benches in the room, people had to stand or sit on the floor. Some people brought blankets or sheep skins to sit on. Because it was dark when we met, the people also entered with their homemade lanterns, usually a can with an opening in the front, a string or wire handle and a candle burning inside or a wick in a smaller can of oil.

The room filled quickly and the smell of the oils from the homespun woolen clothes permeated the room. If it had been raining, everyone would have smelled of wet sheep. To me, the people of this area have always smelled of new potatoes. Nothing was synthetic here. Everyone settled down comfortably as the dust that rose up also settled along with the attendees.

The slides that I had made of that village were the material for the first meeting. I had borrowed a portable generator and a carousel slide projector from other parishes to show the slides. People were not curious about these gadgets but took this hi-tech presence in stride and there was nothing strange about the way I showed the pictures. The purpose of these first meetings was to get people to see themselves, recognize themselves and begin to talk about themselves. The pictures of everyday village life made for a happy, cheerful meeting because the people saw themselves at work in the fields, tending animals, and at home with cooking and other chores.

No details were lost on this earthen screen and everyone enjoyed the show. I asked questions about how they felt to see themselves on a large screen. They said they liked the fact that they could see themselves working and not in a stiff pose before a camera and they liked how they looked. One picture had only the foot of someone who had passed by and did not appear in the picture. Everyone was able to identify the woman just from her shoe. I was amazed at their keen sense of observation, a skill that would help them grasp and discuss issues arising from each meeting. We closed the first meeting with the promise of coming back the following week.

For the second meeting, we showed the same pictures of the village sandwiched between pictures of Inca and Tiahuanaco ruins of their past and pictures of the city of Lima, representing something of their future. The immediate reaction to this showing was anger. They were angry with themselves for being so lazy, ignorant and other characterizations that made them look like bad people. This self-depreciation displayed a chief characteristic of the oppressed.

> So often they hear that they are good for nothing, know nothing and are incapable of learning anything—that they are sick, lazy and unproductive—that in the end they become convinced of their own unfitness.[15]

I really had to intervene and I told them that this was not a meeting to criticize them; they had a glorious past and a promising future and they were in the middle of this flow of life. It was a turning point because together we set up the direction of our future meetings. My visits to the villages for

15. Freire, *Pedagogy,* p. 45

missions and sick calls allowed me to see and experience the hard life of the Aymara villagers. When attending the rituals to Mother Earth, I was up all night participating in the ceremony with the family; I took part in their conversations, heard their concerns and, especially, heard their pleas to the spirits around them.

In their rites for Mother Earth and for the local spirits, they asked for good crops, protection from damaging weather and increase of the animals. They did not ask for too much, asking for only what they needed; asking for more than what offended Mother Earth and the other spirits. With these limits on acquiring wealth, the Aymara remained in a fixed lifestyle of submitting themselves to the instructions of the spirits, and to the demands or limits placed by the non-Indian population, especially local authorities. Although the townspeople saw the Indians as racially inferior, Aymara families made great sacrifices to send their children to school. Even then, families often interrupted that education by having the children help in the fields both in planting and in harvesting crops. There was no apparent effort by teachers to keep the children in school for their own good.

An example of this attitude of little or no education for the children was evident in the town of Platería. When Maryknoll arrived in Puno, Platería was the seat of the Adventist Church in this region. In the 1920's, Fernando Stahl, an American Adventist missionary, wrote a history of his establishing the Adventist missions in Peru. He recounted how the Indians of Platería accepted him and of the consequences they paid for becoming Adventists. As he evangelized this town, he handed out Bibles and told the small congregation to read and talk about what they read. He showed them how to read some passages and held some meetings for reflection and prayer. Then, he would tell the congregation that he was going to visit the mission he had started in Bolivia. When he left, the townspeople from Puno some 15 miles away came to the village and harassed and beat the Aymara for becoming members of this Protestant church; they even jailed a young boy when the intruders could not find his parents.

When the missionary returned, the townspeople disappeared, a routine that happened every time the American went off to the Bolivian mission. The townspeople complained to the bishop that Protestants were moving into the area. At another time, the townspeople actually called for help from the local army base and had the troops beat and intimidate the population of Platería. This congregation remained committed to the American church and functioned independently, reading and reflecting on the Bible. In the course of all this activity, it turned out that the townspeople were fighting to keep the Indians from learning to read.[16] When I arrived in Ilave, most of the rural schoolchildren were learning to read and write. However, what I saw was that even the young people who made it through high school had lost most of their Spanish after they returned to live in their home villages. Those who traveled to the coastal cities to find work often worked as servants, and their limited Spanish made it difficult to find employment.

While our meetings did not address the problem of discrimination, we did set the tone for the Aymara to become part of the larger Peruvian society on their own merits. This kind of accomplishment involved getting people to become aware of themselves in a new light. To arrive at these goals, we used several group dynamics techniques to help the participants express themselves as fully in charge of their own lives, that is, they did not have to conform to the prejudicial images cast on them by the predominant non-Indian culture.

The first two meetings gave people a fresh self-identity; the third meeting consisted of having groups of four or five people draw posters of the village twenty years earlier and another set of posters of the village twenty years into the future. The futuristic posters inevitably included a lijuana, the short handle hoe for harvesting potatoes, and the colorful llijjllas. Each group described the drawings and answered questions about their drawing. They took great pride in their accomplishments. We had begun to let the people learn and speak about some of their dreams and goals. We were witnessing a transformation about how the people thought about themselves without outsiders' judgement of them as unclean and ignorant. In the next meeting, we asked questions about the posters and learned that the things they drew were expensive, like the use of tractors and building multi-story houses. Nonetheless, they wanted this future.

In the fifth meeting, we employed the "fish-bowl" technique in which four members are seated in the middle, surrounded by the audience; they discussed among themselves some of the issues the community faced as they looked to the future. All present listened intensely to what these men were saying. The following meeting had four new members form a panel to field questions from the audience. In both the "fish-bowl" and the panel discussion, there was intense participation by the community because they were fully in charge of the meetings.

In the seventh meeting, we conducted a puppet show. I made some puppets from papier mâché. I practiced the story of the three brothers who were the most dreaded spirits, wind, hail and frost. The dialogue was simple and short for my limited Aymara but the story was clear. After the puppet

16. Stahl, *En el País,* pp. 63–68.

show, I brought out the puppets to the spectators. Many shied away because they thought these were the real spirits, the achachila. People believe the spirits are miniature people and come only when invoked. No one ever sees them because they come in total darkness during the all-night offerings to Mother Earth. The shaman always asked that all present put out the candles and lanterns because the *achachila* were coming to speak to the gathering.

At this meeting, all present thought that I had actually brought the spirits into their view and were afraid; but I assured them, "These are dolls. I made them myself. They are not the *achachila*." I took my hand out from the puppet and showed them how to manipulate them. "They are like a glove," I told them. "Try them out yourselves. Who wants to do a show?"

Immediately, two women volunteered and proceeded to do a roast on the villagers. They had the audience howling with laughter. At the end of the roast, I asked them what they thought of the meeting. They said they enjoyed it immensely and were so happy to have been there. There were no hard feelings from being the butt of the jokes; they were happy with themselves.

As I look back on this particular meeting, I believe I got them thinking about their concept of the *achachila,* because I depicted the dreaded spirits with puppets. For the viewers, these were not puppets; they were spirits themselves. They were afraid that if they saw the spirits, they would damage their eyes. With this show, they could manipulate these spirits without terror or fear of dying. The women who volunteered were able to control these spirits in the puppets.

The eighth meeting was lighthearted with the people very comfortable with themselves as they raised questions and discussed issues the community was trying to resolve; four men simply got up to answer the questions being raised. I got an occasional question, which served to recognize that I was there. I usually turned the question back to them and asked what they would do.

Finally, we came to the last of these meetings. Up to this point, we had viewed pictures of the community, drawn posters, conducted puppet shows and, with each activity, discussed issues about life in the village. For this final meeting, we were showing a Bolivian movie titled: "Ukhamau" ("That's the way it is"). How we got the movie I do not know but we showed it.

Jorge Sanjinés and his filmmakers are Bolivian intellectuals, known as "Grupo Ukamau," who have produced movies in Quechua, Spanish and two in Aymara. Their movies deal with social problems brought into the communities by outsiders, from the time of the conquest to the present. These movies aim at preserving local culture, liberating the people from the throes of racism and social exclusion and creating a new political mentality. For these villagers, this movie fit into the themes of many of our discussions.

Ukhamau is about a young couple, Andrés and Sabina. The young wife is raped and murdered. She manages to tell her husband the name of her attacker before she dies. To show the movie, I borrowed a movie projector and a gas-powered generator. I even had to borrow a Land Rover to be able to carry the generator to this community.

In Anccasaya, the very first village where we viewed this movie, I explained that, unlike other pictures we had seen, these pictures move and the people in them speak Aymara. This was something new! No one seemed impressed with the introduction. I started the movie. The credits began to scroll on our mud wall screen. The audience could not read them and became distracted and, very shortly, carried on loud conversations among themselves.

When Andrés appears on the screen leading his donkey, one man in the gathering noticed him and started yelling at Andrés. Then he got upset because Andrès did not answer his greeting. He complained to all the others and some other men started yelling to get Andrés's attention. This community had never seen a movie before. I was awestruck because this group of people and I were learning how to share each other's lives, past and present, old and modern.

The audience quieted down when they saw the couple conversing between them. Andrés tells Sabina that he will be gone all day. When Sabina asks Andrés to buy her a new skirt, the viewers howl with laughter as if to say, "Fat chance, lady!" Andrés leaves and Sabina returns home to let the animals out to pasture, puts dirt on the potato plants, grooms herself, spins, weaves, and cooks. Sabina is an ideal woman and everyone immediately fell in love with her. The spectators were hooked on the movie. The movie continues with a man from town, Ramos, looking for Andrés. Sabina tells him that he is gone all day. Ramos leers at her and tries to grab her. She escapes but Ramos catches her outside. She struggles with him. The villagers apparently were familiar with a rape. They yelled all kinds of encouragement to Ramos as, "Throw her down," "lift her skirt" and other such things. The women were laughing until Ramos grabs Sabina by the braids and hits her head against a rock.

This blow came as such a shock to the audience that they became completely quiet through to the end of the movie. Even the generator outside the room with its chugging and churning went unnoticed. Sabina lived long enough to tell Andrés who attacked her. At the end Andrés manages to avenge the death of his wife as he meets up with Ramos at an isolated place. Andrés kills Ramos in a long, hand-to-hand, to-the-death fight. At the end, a bruised and bleeding Andrés is standing victorious, panting, with a bloodied rock in his hand. The camera pans away from these two men until they are tiny figures on the screen and the word Ukhamau bursts from the two men and fills the screen. "That's the way it is!" The whole audience seemed able to read the message: Ukhamau!

The audience did not object to this revenge. They did not bring up issues of rape and murder even though they are terrible crimes; besides, rape usually does not end with killing a woman. Everyone seemed stunned as the movie was so close to home in every detail: the houses, the clothing, the food and the language. This was the first showing; I did not know where the movie would take the people. Discussion began immediately among themselves and did not even include me; they knew what to say or do. They did not set out to rebel against the town centers. They simply wanted recognition and respect. The discussion that followed was brief. This community had its cemetery by the side of the road. It is always run down and unkempt. They decided to clean it up, repair the graves and walls and paint the whole cemetery; that way, people who drive or walk by would know this community takes pride in itself. I saw that cemetery afterwards; it is now beautiful, so clean and so bright, a sight so different from any other village and more attractive than the town's cemetery.

Other villages had similar experiences. One village filled in a ravine that was dividing the community through erosion. They pooled their efforts together to fill in that gorge with rocks and dirt and then, they set up a marketplace over that former ravine so that the foot traffic would create firm ground and prevent future possibilities of erosion and division of their community. Another group had their leaders come into town to tell the governor that they were no longer accepting his naming the lieutenant governor for their village. They were going to follow the old tradition of running the village through a tribal council.

The community of Jach'a Winch'occa had lost most of their land to townspeople for small loans they could not pay in time or in full. The townspeople were farming those lands every year for themselves, thereby depriving that village of those crops. They did hire workers from the same village to work the fields and harvest them, only to pay the workers about 25 pounds of potatoes for a day's work. The community decided to throw out the townspeople from their properties, get their lands back, and farm for themselves.

These are but a few examples of decisions that came from the people. All came from nine weeks of meeting, reflecting and acting on the world immediately around them. As a result, these meetings created a certain tension between the townspeople and us, the parish priests. They criticized us as being communists, as spies who did not have any interest in Masses. Our employees often came in to relate these comments about us. Once, they reported that the people wanted to throw us out of town, even tar and feather us. Around this time, the PIP (Policía Investigative de Perú) had called in several priests for interrogation as a way of showing us that the government was very much in charge.

The PIP called me in, too, with instructions to come with several of my best friends. When I asked some catechists and villagers to accompany me, they were afraid of the police. I explained that they were really trying to intimidate us foreigners; furthermore, we had heard that some of the questions involved the citizens as well, especially about how much land they held and number of cattle and other livestock they owned. Rumor had it that the government wanted to find a way to charge new taxes.

We role-played the interview in which they were to speak only Aymara and I was to be their translator. I was to translate every question so that they knew what was going on. When the investigator asked about cattle, they were to remain stone-faced, wait for the translation and then raise a fuss in which they started talking and complaining all at once. Just as we foresaw, the investigator did ask about cattle holdings. In the ensuing confusion of complaints and protests, the detective asked what was happening. I raised my arms to hush the men and asked what was happening to them. Again, all tried to talk at once and I told them to speak one at a time. After hearing each of the men, I translated their complaint: that the police were trying to determine the taxes they could charge the Indians based on their cattle. Once I finished translating, the inquisitor opened the drawer to his desk, pushed the notes he had been taking and said, "This interview is over. You may all go." Very seriously, we made our way out of the police office and went to a nearby store to buy some beer and toast our successfully frustrating interview. Even while we drank our beer, several spies for the PIP kept walking among us to listen to our conversation. Apparently, they were Quechua speaking and did not get much information on us. This incident reflected how the formation of reflection groups apparently had reached the ears of the PIP.

We could now claim that we were able to know the Aymara by recognizing the people and their values, their goals and their achievements, all through the reflection/action groups. This was very different from the church work I had been doing until now. In fact, my own ministry changed quite a bit in that I spent more time visiting the sick. We connected with the spirituality of the Aymara, the spirituality of the *anawim*; we learned that the people had a defining power, a healing power. There was to be no reason for them to fear of being Indian or poor or ignorant because whatever they lacked, God takes the initiative to complete their lives just as I had read in Revelations 21, 5: "The one who sat on the throne said, "Behold, I make all things new.""

The people themselves got to the point at which they knew what to say and what to do. This outcome was liberating as new leaders surfaced, an achievement for which they deserve full credit. This was the result of taking the people and their culture seriously taking the time to speak with them in their cultural environment. They, in turn, appeared to have moved away from the saint-Catholicism as they no longer asked for fiesta Masses or blessing crying babies and other requests I had heard in my earlier ministry.

My grasp of the Aymara's beliefs seemed sufficient to create reflection groups based on their values and faith. All ministry is not simply taking care of people but of giving them a vision of a time in which there is a transformation and a unity among peoples, an age in which all realize themselves as the people of God. In my sermons about the poor, I turned to Isaiah 65, 17—23:

> Lo, I am about to create new heavens and a new earth; the things of the past shall not be remembered or come to mind. Instead, there shall always be rejoicing and happiness in what I create;
> . . . No longer shall the sound of weeping be heard there, or the sound of crying; No longer shall there be in it an infant who lives but a few days or an old man who does not round out his full lifetime;
> . . . They shall live in houses they build, and eat the fruits of the vineyards they plant. . .
> . . . They shall not toil in vain nor beget children for sudden destruction; For a race blessed by the lord are they and their offspring. Before they call, I will answer; while they are speaking, I will hearken to them. The wolf and the lamb shall graze alike, and the lion shall eat hay like the ox. . . . None shall hurt or destroy on my holy mountain, says the Lord.

Isaiah's words convey the Christian notion of history as linear and that God intervenes in history, thereby, preventing us from being simply passive recipients of God's miracles; we interact with God in forging history toward the end times, toward the eschatological age. From within the culture of the Aymara, we began to forge the history of the Aymara.

6

Symbolic Language of the Aymara

"A symbol also unlocks dimensions and elements of our soul which correspond to the dimensions and elements of reality. A great play gives us not only a new vision of the human scene, but it opens up hidden depths of our own being."

—PAUL TILLICH, DYNAMICS OF FAITH

ORGANIZING THE ACTION-REFLECTION GROUPS involved several contributing factors, and the basis for their success lay in the understanding and use of symbolic language. We need to discuss symbol for the following reasons. First, symbol allows us to enter into a new culture since each culture has many mechanisms in symbolic form that identify this people as Aymara or whatever culture in which they live. Second, symbol is what restores good order to one's life or resolves some problem or inner conflict in one's life or that of a community. Third, the familiarity with and the use of traditional symbols obliges the missionary or change agent to create new symbols. This chapter, therefore, deals with the steps toward identifying symbols that define the way of life of a people. The examples presented in this chapter often go back to ritual elements we saw in previous chapters; but here we will put them in perspective with both the beliefs and the lifestyle of the Aymara.

Beginning with the task of identifying a culture, the missionary faces a great challenge. Generally, seminary preparation for mission work usually consisted of learning theology so thoroughly that the future task for priests appeared to be one of maintaining orthodoxy and right moral conduct. Intercultural training was non-existent except for a summer course in introductory linguistics. Therefore, we missionaries ended up teaching or preaching the facts of faith from the catechism; we had Aymara villagers memorize questions and answers about Catholic faith in order to reward them with confessions, Mass and the Eucharist. How did we know whether people found something meaningful in this parroted type of learning? Most of us missionaries learned our faith as children from the catechism but we were already members of a faith community. What we needed from these villagers was the experience of faith, a meaningful encounter with God. The symbolic language in the Aymara rituals allowed us to understand these ceremonies as meetings with the hill spirits and with God; an experience that gives the participants a feeling of satisfaction and fulfillment, something I could understand from my own religious experience.

We missionaries began our mission with goals of converting people to Christianity and of providing them pastoral care. Once at our mission station, we were exposed to a wholly different world. The landscape, the stores, the food and the language were all different. We met people of a different culture, who wore different clothes, which gave them their own smell. However, we missionaries depended on hired help to guide us through drivable fields, to do the shopping, to cook to our tastes and to interpret for us. It was as if we were not living in the real world, and so we created one that looked like ours. Nonetheless, simply learning Spanish was a strong indicator of delving into a new culture; for example, the formality with which parishioners received priests, in contrast to how they greet each other with hugs; requesting Masses for patronal saints in contrast to having Mass celebrated in memory of deceased relatives was new to us. Speaking Spanish alone did not introduce us to the symbolic language of the Aymara rituals that were meetings with the spirits, the achachila, and with God. These symbols had their beginnings in the long history of the Aymara. Catholics can relate to centuries of symbols, evolving into the Mass of today. The wise men of those times formulated for the people symbols that allowed them to communicate with the spirits and with the spiritual environment in their lives. The mountains and hills were already there and they took on names to identify them as specific spirits; communicating with them was the way to deal with life, however harsh and unrewarding it could be. In a sense, this explains how a people can live and survive at or above the tree line and cultivate foodstuffs on apparently unrewarding land. The weather is consistently harsh and often destructive, but their spirit guides them through a myriad of hardships and they reap harvests regularly.

However, there is more to symbol than just religious experiences; it takes one into the heart of a culture we would not know without symbolic language or action, religious or secular. British anthropologist, Victor Turner, in his book, *The Ritual Process,* helped me put ritual practices into a context broader than religion:

> Rituals reveal values at their deepest level. . . . Men express in ritual what moves them most, and since the form of expression is conventionalized and obligatory, it is the values of the group that are revealed. I see in the study of rituals the key to an understanding of the essential constitution of human societies.[1]

The Aymara have created their identity within this dialogue between them and the spirits; they reveal their lifestyle. After observing and participating in the rites of the Aymara, I found Turner's observation pertinent to the culture of the townspeople as well; the value systems for the *campesino* and the *misti* are very much the same when it comes to feeling secure and assured of success by performing the same *salud misa.* The split between Indian and non-Indian is a conscious act to discriminate in spite of the unifying characteristics of their rites. Catholic ritual suffers the same effect in which oppressive landowners and socially excluded natives of that area receive the Eucharist that unites them into a fellowship.

Turner further clarifies that the differences among men are not unbridgeable because those differences manifest a broad variety of cultural experiences. Bridging and understanding, meeting and sharing are the actions of community, made up of natives and outsiders. Turner quotes Martin Buber often and recalls how Buber has described this interchange:

> Through the Thou a person becomes I. When two people relate to each other authentically and humanly, God is the electricity that surges between them.[2]

Our rites, the church, the Bible, and the Mass put us in contact with God so that what comes from our innermost self is the love of God. The Aymara rituals that realize this contact with God and the spirits emerge from a loving concern for a sick family member and for the whole community affected by its ill member. Martin Buber describes the kind of environment in which people of different religions or outlooks meet as authentic.

> It is not necessary to know something about God in order really to believe in Him: many true believers know how to talk *to* God

1. Turner, *The Ritual,* p.6.
2. Buber, *I and Thou,* p. 126.

but not *about* Him. If one dares to turn toward the unknown
God, to go to meet Him, to call to Him, Reality is present.[3]

This view of reality comes through symbol and symbolic language
because symbol is something that stands for an idea, an image, a belief,
another reality that we can call spiritual and is not limited to religion. It
can be an event as well as an object that gives a person or group a sense of
wholeness and determination, because symbol connects us to the transcen-
dent elements of our everyday life. A symbol is not a sign of something like
a stop sign or a name of a building, like a library; these identify a traffic
maneuver or a place we visit. A symbol is not the result of a consensus or
agreement, but appears spontaneously in familiar settings. For example, a
flag identifies a country, but for the soldier or the parents of a serviceman,
this flag symbolizes a man's putting his life on the line in defense of his
country and for his parents, a strong sense of patriotism. These are not two
realities, one nearby, the symbol, and another that is far away or intangible.
These two aspects of the same reality resolve something that is unsettling
to a person or to a community. In the attached table are a list of situations
that are disconcerting for the Aymara, the effects of those concerns, and
the remedies the Aymara use to resolve those conflicts, thereby restoring
harmony to their lives. As my CPE supervisor, Bob Cholke, pointed out:

> . . . a symbol points to, or posits, the problem of a specific
> unknown. It is usually precipitated by a crisis due to a lack of
> understanding. It is spontaneous, a function of the unconscious
> dilemma and communicated directly to the ego in the form of a
> felt sense of inspiration.[4]

The table below lists some of those threats to the Aymara, how they
affect them and the ritual steps they take to confront them; the rites with
their symbols help make sense of whatever challenge or confusion they experience. This sense of inspiration comes from these rites and is part of the
cultural identity of the Aymara. From the time of the first missionaries to
this day, the outsider considered these practices superstitious, diabolical, or
simply ignorant. Even the townspeople, the mistis, described the Aymara
as superstitious, even while practicing some of their rites. When I began
observing the ceremonies of the Aymara, my worry was that devil worship
could be involved. On the contrary, these rites are life-preserving acts for
the Aymara; outsiders need this level of cultural awareness to communicate
effectively with the people they serve. To judge the people as ignorant of our

3. Buber, *Eclipse*, p. 40.
4. Cholke, letter to author, May 5, 1972.

world vision is to miss who they are, and how they have lived well enough to survive centuries of life.

Perceived Threats Resolved By Rituals

Threat	Outcome/danger	Action to Resolve Threat
Illnesses	Whole community suffers	Perform a healing rite, a salud misa
Drought	Loss of crops and animals	Prayer vigil on hilltop with children and toads
Enemies/ property disputes	Prolonged and expensive legal battle	Surrender enemy to Mother Earth
Unbaptized babies	Loss of crops to the elements	Baptize live baby; argue to have deceased baby baptized
Alferado expenses	Extravagant expense in sponsoring a fiesta, in return for prominence.	All-night prayer vigil on hilltop
Punishment by Mother Earth	Loss of crops	Sprinkle (*challar*) a libation on the ground at social gatherings

These ritual actions do provide a healing of the anxieties that disrupt the daily life of the Aymara. I have observed children who were healed and some who were not. Likewise, I do not know whether these ceremonies thwarted or dissipated incoming hailstorms or stopped men from being unfaithful; but once people performed these rituals as a healing of sorts, people were confident to face whatever beset them because they were in touch with the spiritual forces of nature. They understood that their spiritual side connected with those spirits, who were not necessarily deities, but they participated in a dialogue of spirit-to-spirit.

In a secular society like that of the United States, the birthplace of most Maryknoll Missionaries, there are no signs of gratitude to Mother Earth with a sprinkling of wine or beer, or a reconciliation through a fixed ceremony; no rites or practices that can stave off hurricanes, earthquakes or drought or any threat from nature. In an oversimplified observation, it seems that in North America, perceived threats come from ruptured relationships among family members, associates and friends or in business dealings. When these relations are broken, the remedy usually consists of seeing someone, a counselor, a friend or a lawyer. Whether these contacts repair the spiritual disruption one suffers is a question to consider, since there are no rituals to resolve these conflicts. However, rituals like celebrating a new birth, birthdays, weddings and even funerals keep relationships strong and people celebrate them to maintain those relationships. Each ethnic group living in America has their own celebrations to maintain stability among themselves and their families. Those who follow a religion have a number of symbols that help them make sense of life, in spite of the limits of our awareness of symbolic expression.

Nonetheless, there are symbols for everyday life. For example, a wedding band on one's finger creates a new lifestyle for the couple; a man is no longer a carefree bachelor but cares for his spouse and family. The ring is a symbol of the married state.

However, in the Ilave area where I worked, I did observe that women take charge through a ritual exercised by misti women when they discover that their husbands or lovers are unfaithful. The ritual consists of smoking three cigarettes tied together while looking intensely on an image of St. Jerome who is sitting with a large book on his lap and a lion at his feet.[5] The woman conducting this procedure draws on the cigarettes and blows the smoke to her right; then, looking at the picture of her husband/lover, she says, "If you are on my right, come back, come back" while fanning the smoke toward her. She does the same to her left, to the front and to the back, each time calling her beloved to return. By now, the ash on the cigarette is long; she turns back to St. Jerome and says, "Just like you were able to bring this lion to your feet, bring back my husband (or lover) to kneel at my feet." She flicks the cigarette ash angrily on the floor and fiercely stomps on the ashes while saying, "Come back, fall at my feet like that lion, you good for nothing so and so" (the words are not as tame as I portray here) and continues to stomp angrily on the ashes. She vents her anger by repeating these actions until there is no more cigarette to burn. Each participant I interviewed about this practice said their husbands/lovers came back repentant and submissive to their women. The woman was successful; this ritual confirmed her strength and control of her life.

A symbol cannot be constructed on a whim or as an indicator, but it can be conventionalized as people follow the same ritual year after year. Unlike symbol, I can put up a For Sale sign and it only indicates a possible transaction. On the other hand, symbols have the unique power to unify unsettling human feelings, thoughts, and experiences into a coherent formation of daily living. Since the spirits are firmly established into the world

---

5. St. Jerome is credited with translating the Hebrew Bible into Latin known as the Vulgate.

in which the Aymara live, connecting and communicating with the spirits and the forces of nature make life worth living for the Aymara. They identify themselves as a people even in their language; a good example is the word to carry. Twenty-four words mean carry, as in the hand, on one's back or shoulder and twenty-one other forms of carrying. These words were not lost or did not disappear from the language when the Spanish colonists introduced the wheel; the twenty-four ways of carrying identify the Aymara!

In their social interaction, the Aymara want a unified people and frequently exercise some form of reconciliation, as in Carnival, or Mardi Gras; the Spanish settlers reveled before the Lenten fasts; whereas the Aymara visit neighbors to ask pardon for any offenses to their neighbor. At the same time, they celebrate the origin of the potato.

For Catholics, the Mass is the symbol of the sacrifice Christ made to free us from sin and punishment; we do not see the act of Christ but the Mass is the sacrifice of Christ that makes our lives meaningful. Also, when a priest visits a person who is dying, the act may not make sense to onlookers, but they can go beyond the priest's visit to the sick as an image of the meaning of life and death, thereby bringing together the known and the unknown. In short, symbol stands for an intangible element that shapes our everyday life into a meaningful life.

The peculiarity of symbols is that they appear and are used without a second thought because they are spontaneous expressions that bring order into people's lives. People have to do the symbolic thing, period! When a woman with her baby on her back moves about in large crowds or visits a church, she leaves that environment fanning her baby's cap as if signaling someone toward her. She is guiding her baby's soul toward her so that it will not be lost or stolen by some spirit. She feels a sense of relief from this gesture. When people gather for a social event and drinks are served, the guests pour out a bit of his/her drink on the ground as a libation to mother earth; they remove their hats out of respect for the source of their food and livelihood.

The symbolism surrounding the death of a family member consoles the family and provides a practical approach to deal with the grief of losing a loved one and the daily responsibilities that befall a family. A person is usually buried the day after death with a viewing in which the favorite foods of the deceased are served to give strength to the soul for its journey; added to this table are drinks and coca leaves for strength. A coin is placed in the mouth of the body and a small broom is tucked inside the shirt or burial tunic; the coin pays off debts and the broom allows the soul to begin a three-year journey by performing the humble task of sweeping which allows the new soul entrance into the afterworld. No one could explain the three-year wait; however, this is the usual length of time to heal that grief.

More impressive is the eight-day ceremony in which the clothes of the deceased are laid out in the patio as if the body were laid out. The family all gather in front of these clothes and face east toward the setting sun. All pray, weep, and mourn loudly. At a given point, the shaman or pacco orders the family to move to the opposite side of the patio and thereby face in the direction of the rising sun. As the people stand up, they remove the black outer garments, ponchos and shawls, shake them vehemently; this is to shake off the grief they are experiencing. When they take their places facing the direction of the rising sun, they are more alert and talkative. They pray for a short while and then get up to watch the burning of the dead person's clothes. They watch the flames intensely as the shadows and figures within the fire cast silhouettes of those who will die next. That worrisome impression has its ritual remedy. Arriaga describes this funeral practice carried out back in 1620.[6]

The mourners return to the patio to be served a bowl of sheep head soup; as they settle about the patio, the conversations get lively and everyone wants to see who gets the eye of the sheep in their soup. That person places the eye on the patio huaca stone and everyone gets to lob stones with their left hands at the eye until it bursts. Whoever is splattered with the juices of the eye is destined to die. The host family brings out a black sheep skin and the attendees take tufts of wool, spin it into thread and wrap that thread around a piece of fat. Then they place those wool balls at the edges of a grain or potato field, anywhere a field mouse can take it. This act takes the threat of death from the attendees whose shadows appeared in the earlier fire and from those who were splattered with juices from the sheep's eye. There are many other symbolic activities related to a death that extend over three years, but this one impressed me most as it is an immediate dispelling of the grief that can interrupt the chores of daily life and ease the pain of the loss of a member of this community.

Other common practices consist of stringing up a dried llama fetus and eggshells over a doorway to ward off the *anchanchu,* an evil night spirit. Designs on their weavings represent the potato fields. The huaca kala, the patio stone, has a place in every home and is a significant symbol that connects this household to the protective spirits of that locality. Each village also has a huaca at the perimeter of the village where offerings to mother earth are burned. The huaca can be compared to Catholics having a picture or painting of Jesus, or the Virgin Mary, or other saints; these images

6. Arriaga, *Extirpation,* p. 76.

connect the family to the spiritual world much like the huaca connects the Aymara to their spirit world. No instruction or Catholic practice have made the huaca disappear from people's lives. All these words, values, norms, beliefs, actions and artefacts make the life of the Aymara meaningful as they are symbols of unseen elements of their culture and are part of daily life.

Even in adversity, when an Aymara suffers harm, like a robbery of animals or property, he or she avoids a lifelong litigation and resorts to symbolic vengeance in which the spirits mete out the punishment. Maria Tapia, seller of ritual elements, told me that her house had been ransacked and she knew who the thief was. She angrily told me she was going to punish him with a curse rite. Since I had seen enough ritual ceremonies to know no devil worship was involved, I asked her if I could attend the ceremony. As it turned out, I did not have access to the ceremony and missed witnessing the symbolism of a curse.

Eight days later, as I was walking home from school with a crowd of students, up ahead we saw a large crowd and I was to pass by them. When I approached this gathering, some students told me that a young man had just collapsed before them; he was unconscious but breathing. I recognized him as the man whom Maria wanted to curse. The young man was swelling noticeably before our eyes. I told the family that he had had a curse on him; I told them to do a *cuti misa*, to counteract the curse. The family suddenly moved away from the unconscious man as if his ailment was contagious and were visibly frightened. They did nothing and the next day they informed me that the man had died. This was quite scary and hardly a religious act.

Another revenge ritual consists of a family having a pacco curse an "enemy" to death by creating a packet of incense, llama fat, bits of clothing or even threads, hair and anything belonging to the cursed one; these elements are placed in a hole at a cross shrine usually on the side of a hill. These rites, whether for good or for bad, helped me understand the dynamic processes contained in these actions. The Aymara feel they exert some power in these dialogues between man and the forces of nature.

When the Aymara celebrate the feast of their village patron saint, they elect a sponsor, the *alferado,* to organize and cover the cost of the fiesta; in spite of a large expense to him, the alferado gains honor and respect along with the responsibility to maintain good order. When Marcelino and I talked about wealth, about God and about good behavior, he told me,

> These sponsors (alferados) receive a whip during this fiesta. This whip is a sign of authority. This new authority can keep order in the fiesta as well as for the year he serves as *alferado.* This symbol of the whip is a step toward maintaining justice and the position

demands prayer. The way to pray is to go up a hilltop with a bowl
of burning incense. There the person needs to be naked to pray.
This is the way to be close to God.[7]

While rites are the common ground on which Christian beliefs and
Aymara spirits' religiosity meet, the symbolism is not necessarily religious.
We missionaries come to realize that we are not bringing God as a package
of unknown goods. Neither are we giving people something they do not
have. God is here. We find God in this dialogue.

> One does not find God if one remains in the world; one does not
> find God if one leaves the world. Whoever goes forth to his You
> with his whole being and carries to it all the being of the world,
> finds him whom one cannot seek.[8]

When we meet with the people, we establish a meaningful rapport
with them through symbolic language that is in keeping with the local culture. Each culture creates its own world of symbols; they are not like abstract
axioms to be applied to a culture but created to form a communication of
culture. We go into a different sphere of understanding the world around
us. In short, this is how I saw the Aymara religion, namely, as a subject for
reflection, not investigation for its strangeness; also, its proliferated challenges impelled me to create or use new symbols. Sermons, in particular,
I found to be a strongly effective way in which we can apply our knowledge of the spiritual world of the Aymara and of townspeople who share
the same values and beliefs. In a sermon, we try not to bluff the people or
ourselves. An Aymara has not tried to deceive anyone by acting out what he
believes. In this context, religion is a way of life and not a studied description of unknown things, or a set of rites that can delude the people. I am
reminded of a story, *San Manuel Bueno*[9] by Miguel Unamuno in which a
self-declared atheist accompanied his family to Mass regularly. All he got
out of the services was material with which to criticize the religion. Then
one time, he listened closely to the priest's praying the *credo* with the people.
He made the declaration of faith with the people until he got to the closing
of the Creed: "I believe in the Holy Spirit, the communion of saints and . . ."
and his voice trailed off so as not to say "the resurrection of the body." The
atheist picked up on that detail and went to visit the priest to discuss his
observation. After some discussion, the priest admitted that he had doubts
about life after death. They discussed this point at length with the result

7. Salazar, Unpublished manuscript, May 19, 1971.

8. Buber, *I and Thou*, p. 127.

9. Unamuno, *San Manuel*, pp. 228–244.

that the atheist became close friends with the priest. He even reconciled himself with the church and began to receive the sacraments. The priest could not delude this atheist and in his honesty regained this man back into the church, doubts and all.

I used this story at a funeral service of a townsperson because the men who attended were strongly anti-clerical, an attitude they saw as a strong value. I linked the story to Jesus's raising Lazarus from the dead (John 11, 1—44). Jesus told Martha, "Your brother will rise." When she reiterated her belief in the "resurrection on the last day," Jesus was telling her to believe now in rising from the dead. Faith is demanded now, not for some future event; living by what we believe takes place now. One man approached me after the funeral and said, "This is real preaching. This is what we need." Symbolic language was very much at work.

Sermons are the verbal symbols from which we all experience a sense of direction and purpose. I recall another sermon about trusting in God, which gave my listeners and me a sense of inspiration and vision. Jesus's parables apply closely to life in these highlands of Peru. Life is harsh and many times the food gets scarce until the next harvest. This state is called *jakejj jalanta,* the time of need for people, a condition that can last from October to May. When they hear that God cares enough to feed the birds, they understand that God cares for them more than he cares for birds. Even animals suffer scarcity during the months from June to December. This is called *uywa jalanta.*

The homily was based on the reading from Matthew 6, 25–34, in which Jesus told his followers "Do not worry about your life, what you will eat or drink, or about your body, what you will wear. . . Look at the birds in the sky; they do not sow or reap, they gather nothing into barns, yet your heavenly Father feeds them. Are you not more important than they?" People do rely on God, or the local spirits, to pull them through difficult times. I described to them that confidence in God is like a woman going across an open field with her baby on her back. A pack of dogs comes out of nowhere to attack her. The woman bends down to pick up rocks to throw at the attacking dogs. The baby swings down with a mother's movement and gurgles with laughter as if the mother's stooping down is a game. The baby does not even feel the danger around him in the safety of that colorful llijjlla. This is how to confide in God, like a child in his mother's care. The sermon was on target with its symbolic message. The catechists loved this sermon and retold it repeatedly in the villages because it reflected their life and the dangers they face every day; it also touched their spirituality. This is one example of how the people taught me to appreciate and feel the impact of gospel stories and their place in the world of the Aymara symbols.

In using and creating symbols, as in our sermons, we appreciate the use of symbolic acts and gestures; the Aymara teach us that symbol is not solely religious but takes one into the spiritual elements in their lives. As we connect with the spiritual, whether hill spirits or praying in church, or celebrating a birthday or name day, called *día del santo*, we find the spiritual in all of life activities making our lives whole and fulfilling. Even in the relatively few symbols in American life, these symbols, gestures and celebrations make our life complete, ordered and meaningful. The birth of a child, baptisms or christenings and birthdays all celebrate life and are celebrated enthusiastically as these occasions are an expansion of the family line and life. All of these occasions celebrate life, much as the Aymara rites extend life. In our sermons, we need to convey what is profound in people's lives rather than explain doctrinal correctness.

To be in touch with the profound, I suggest that we dream, first, about ourselves. Dream about how we will be successful as a missionary. Imagine ourselves conversing in a new language about what people find important. Let ourselves go and express those dreams to others about what we want to say and do. Have it all come out of our inner self. Those vivid dreams give us direction for sharing what we have and what brought us to this strange country, to speak a strange language about the things that make sense to us and to the communities we serve. This same technique keeps us from the stagnancy of repeated acts. Symbolic language gives one the power to be creative.

7

Reflections on Change Transformations

"Everything depends on inner change; when this has taken place,
then, and only then does the world change."

—MARTIN BUBER

The reflection groups did create a noticeable change in the Aymara participants. Part of the transformation came from having the people reflect on
their own reality. As a result, the Aymara broke the mold into which the early Spanish colonists and then the *misti* had placed them, namely, that they
were inferior and that they brought this condition of ignorance, poverty and
isolation on themselves. Whenever government officials visited a local village, the Aymara spokesperson always began with the same words: "Señores
autoridades, estamos jodidos" "Gentlemen authorities, we are screwed."
For these visiting experts, the Aymara could not think beyond farming
potatoes, wearing homespun clothes and speaking their own language
rather than Spanish. It was hard to see what help the authorities provided
for these villages. Likewise, no misti saw themselves allowing the Aymara
any alternative from their village life and subsistence farming. In contrast,
these reflection groups helped the people discover alternatives, which they

themselves defined and carried out, or as Freire states, the people found the words to describe their new reality.[1]

The reflection groups started as part of the pastoral care we were providing. Since the people knew me as a priest of the parish, these meetings were seen as a work of the Church. I had opted to follow Freire's model for reflection groups which Gutierrez's describes as:

> They thus make the transfer from a naïve awareness which does not deal with problems, gives too much value to the past, tends to accept mythical explanations, and tends toward debate—to a critical awareness—which delves into problems, is open to new ideas, replaces magical explanations with real causes, and tends to dialogue.[2]

This language was to come out of their cultural view of reality, which we learned from their rituals and from long visits to the villages. Also, we wanted to avoid the kind of imposition as described in the works of Arriaga, Huaman Poma and other chroniclers when the Catholic faith was forced on the newly conquered people with public punishments for those who resisted.[3] Early Spanish missionaries like Antonio de Montesinos and Bartolomé de las Casas denounced the harsh abuse and enslavement of the indigenous people of the Americas. The Aymara did not need history lessons to recall the abuse and persecution they had suffered at the hands of the Spanish colonists and missionaries for whom Catholicism was the official religion and the basis of culture. The Catholic religion that the missionaries had brought to the new world was good, but the cases surrounding imposing it and the history of abuse in enforcing it made me reflect on how we could approach a new culture.

Do we approach the study of other cultures with the idea that there is something to be gained by it? Does our learning about the people give us a headway for working effectively in our mission? These questions reveal our short sightedness. Finding some advantage over others is like being an animal of prey, in search of game, looking for something to devour. We appear to be voracious and hungry when we approach other peoples. But, as we bite and break the outer shell, we should not expect to be filled. It can never be the sole enrichment of one party. The result should be a mutual enrichment in our melding into the Aymara culture. We should expect to be swallowed up so that we are both the food and the consumer. Both become one in absorbing another culture and people. Both are lost, yet revealed in

1. Freire, *Pedagogy,* p. 15.

2. Gutierrez, *A Theology* p. 57.

3. Arriaga, *Extirpation,* p. 128; and Huaman Poma, *A Letter,* p. 144.

the oneness of that meeting. We give up our ambitions of dominating and we find a new person. The Aymara found a new Aymara and I detected a new me. What emerged was community, a deeply spiritual experience for me. My faith tells me this is what Christ did in his coming into the world. He so entered into being human that he also revealed and made room for communion and community. He went back to the Father because he died and rose from the dead, not because his community ended.

Another result of the action-reflection group meetings surprised me in the sense that I did not know what to expect; the people knew what they wanted from this experience. The people were the decision makers in the projects they created. The role I had played as priest did not enter into what they were going to say or do. This was not a moral performance nor was it a clamoring for a blessing or for baptizing a dead child. Somehow, they broke from what they traditionally requested. The people came to treat me differently. This was borne out when a member of the Canadian Agricultural mission asked me to make a presentation about a plow they had developed. This plow needed little power, oxen or human, to open the earth. The Canadian volunteer explained how to use this plow and how its curvature would make plowing easier than the traditional wooden plow. We went to a community I had never visited where he introduced me. A man from the gathering got up and told the people: "Listen to this man. He has something to tell you." Apparently, my reputation of working with communities preceded me. Also, this was an unusual comment as most villagers simply listen to an outsider with little or no response. Generally, they have no opinion about the value of a presentation. Now they were more decisive about what to hear out and what to decide as good for their community.

The Maryknoll missionaries' discovering many details of the Aymara religion produced some modifications at Mass, provided a more focused spiritual care and continued to improve the quality of life with programs in healthcare, education, and leadership training. We considered ourselves agents of change with regard to the physical needs of the people. As for the spiritual needs, the approach now included acknowledging that the Aymara express spirituality in their beliefs and rituals, something we could now identify. Here is where the people were able to see our ministry as vital to their lives. While we were formulating this pastoral care, more priests began speaking Aymara more frequently than I had observed in my first few years in the parish of Ilave. Arriaga had pointed out in the 1680's that the biggest obstacle to evangelization and to rooting out idolatry was ignorance of the language.[4]

---

4. Arriaga, *Extirpation*, pp 62, 160.

Another innovation happened in Chucuito, where the tireless missionary, Fr. Francis T. McGourn, founded and operated the Institute for Aymara Studies with a staff well prepared in both the Aymara language and Aymara ways of life. Together with this team, Fr. Francis produced 32 tracts on Aymara beliefs, customs and social structures. These were published at the Institute and distributed to all the priests in the area to enhance their missionary efforts. They even produced an Aymara translation of the liturgy. Other than the catechism and the Aymara New Testament from the Bible Society of Bolivia, there had been no other religious literature in Aymara.

In Bolivia, Fr. John Gorski, also a Maryknoll priest, wrote several treatises on the theology of culture. His writings and his expertise earned him the position of executive secretary of the mission department of the Latin American Bishops' Conference from 1975 to 1979. He enjoyed the title of Missiologist/Theologian.[5]

Maryknoll in Peru even hired a husband and wife team of social anthropologists to provide a professional evaluation of the new revision of the indigenous mission in Peru. All these works were the result of our becoming aware of the specific religiosity of the Aymara; our approach to people was a more comprehensive way with speaking the local language, recognizing the people's ancient religion and fitting these attitudes within our mission goals.

I, too, changed drastically. First, I fell in love with a people to the point that I felt I wanted to stay with the community and spend the rest of my life among them. I even started toying with the idea of getting married. The only reason for this kind of thinking was that, for the Aymara, the only mature person is a married man who speaks with authority in these communities. My dominion as a priest was an official one and was called upon in specific situations. But a married man has a more authentic influence to contribute to the function and future of the community. The priest only provided ritual duties that confirmed the religious practices carried out by the people. Since four other priests with whom I had worked in this parish had left to marry, the idea of marrying was not all that new or strange to me. It was simply the closeness to the people that put the idea of marrying into my head. Besides, I had no partner in mind and the people closest to me were the Sisters who work with us. I did not even know where to begin in looking for a wife. At first, I began by asking each of the Sisters if they wanted to stay in Peru. Anyone of them could have been my wife. Besides I needed a partner for my work. Each and every one simply said no. In fact, they were ready to leave Peru at a moment's notice. This had not been an easy mission for them. That was the end of my "courtship." What I was really trying to resolve was how

5. Gorski, "How the Catholic", pp. 60–64.

to dedicate my life to this community. I felt very much at home with the people and saw their future as part of my life. I had an agenda and perhaps marrying would help me complete that agenda.

Then it happened. I had asked Trinidad to assist me with these meetings especially when it came to speaking with the women; I felt they were the real force for any kind of change. What had happened was that in the villages, according to custom, men and women sat separately in the room. One evening I made a mistake of going to the women's side to address my remarks to them. The following meeting, the women were absent. So, Trinidad was the person to help us addressing the women and she agreed. I informed the villagers that a woman was coming to talk to them. I could not ask the Sisters from the parish to help me, as they did not know Aymara.

Trinidad was a natural for these meetings and discussions. She answered lots of questions and facilitated lengthy discussions. She was familiar with the kinds of ideas we were discussing and developing in these meetings. She was so good that she could have conducted a meeting on her own.

Her greatest contribution came when we were getting ready for a meeting. At that time, I used to smoke cigarettes, often as many as three packs a day and had smoked for eighteen years. While we were loading our equipment on to the car, I was coughing a lot. Trinidad looked at me and said, "You're smoking too much. What happens to us if you get sick?" I heard one word and something happened. I put out my cigarette and have not smoked since that day. The word "us" resonated in my head and in my heart. Something clicked. At the same moment that I stopped smoking, I realized that I had been in love with Trinidad all along but had never let that sentiment surface. I even saw her as possibly part of the rest of my life. I had first met her eleven years earlier and only now did I take her seriously.

Even though I felt I had focused on the woman who could possibly be my wife, I did not blurt out what I sensed that evening. I wanted to see if she were free to marry since she had been married before. I did not express my feelings for her at that moment as I had a new task at hand: was Trinidad available? If so, I would begin to court her.

This is really strange because I thought I had put the notion of marrying pretty much out of my mind. This thought and this feeling took me by surprise. Now I had a reason to marry and incorporate myself into the Aymara community. If she were free to marry and if she accepted me, I would ask for the necessary dispensations to be released from the vows of chastity and obedience and from my ministerial and church duties. But I faced two obstacles. The first was that Trinidad had been married before and abandoned 10 years earlier by Silvestre, her first husband. Rumors had circulated frequently that Silvestre had died on the coast. Now, these rumors caught my attention. If I were to marry, it would have to be in the church because I wanted the sacraments for the rest of my life. Even though I felt this intense love for her, I wanted to make sure that we could marry in the church.

The other obstacle was my being an outsider, a foreigner, and Trinidad had no way of investigating my family background. Still, I felt that with this decision, I was on my way to being a spokesman for the Aymara and for other native groups who are the most oppressed and the most removed from the mainstream of society.

From appreciating how the scriptures spoke to the people here, I felt I owed the community greater permanency. Permanency meant a long-range project, something like that of the translators of the Bible Society, who spend years being with people in unexplored regions, learning the language, creating a grammar and dictionary and eventually providing a Bible in their language.[6] They do not move away to carry out such a project but stay in that region. There is so much credibility in that kind of dedication on the part of the Bible translators. Their motive is that the word of God gives life. This is not an academic or research task nor a way of beating out other Christian sects to take hold of the people. They simply possessed the kind of faith and commitment to enter and stay in some primitive settings to bring the word of God to unnoticed and invisible people. Along with translating the Bible in the people's language, they are promoting literacy and a new approach to life. For example, the Canadian Baptists in Bolivia produced a Bible in Aymara along with religious and folk literature in written form. I was moved by those kinds of efforts and accomplishments. This new vision of my wanting to stay with this community, for me, was highly spiritual.

I had the advantage, as a Catholic priest, of living in a spirit world and guiding people in spiritual matters. The Aymara also live by a world of spirits. That similar environment readied me for dealing with the spiritual element of their lives. Those who do not live with an awareness of the spirit world would find working with the Aymara as guess work. The notion that spirits run people's lives is abhorrent to outsiders. The visitor has to be practical with hands-on, measurable works. Relating to people becomes even harder to accomplish because, for such workers, spirits do not act and are not considered real. Effort is best put into providing for people's health care, their education, leadership training, community projects, and providing some economic help. All these kinds of projects seem to put the spiritual into a secondary position. We can easily get a response from the people with schools, clinics, and catechetical training. These are attractive programs, but how long will the effect of these programs last in the lives of the people?

6. Feu, *The Bible*, pp. 311–315.

I saw Peace Corp volunteers set up projects to help with farming methods. The German bishops financed an elaborate machine shop with excellent tools and projects to help the people. There were agricultural missions and the purchase of a fine breed of sheep to help the people. But as volunteers left, these shops and programs were closed shut until the next volunteer group showed up. These projects did not seem to survive as part of the people's lives. Getting this kind of international aid to the people often faces challenges or even opposition because of the people's focus on asking the spirits what to do.

Another obstacle comes from the suspicion people have that the foreigner comes to study the people or to dominate them. This two-fold opposition was dramatized in a 1969 Bolivian movie called, "Yawar Mallku." The story was about American members of Cuerpo del Progreso, a weakly disguised Peace Corp, who operated an obstetric clinic. They were sterilizing unsuspecting women of a village as a means to better their economic development, and, in a subtle way, to eliminate an inferior race. The movie included rock and roll music in the sound track and showed the volunteers distributing American-style clothes to the people in place of their traditional homespun.

The film reflected a common notion in Latin countries in the 1960's that American cultural imperialism was present to overcome them; this concept included missionaries as part of this imperialism. Many told me that their first impression of Maryknoll missionaries was that they were soldiers preparing for a greater attack on this region.

Still I wanted to stay as a member of this community. I had no problem with the lack of amenities I had known in the United States as well as in the parish house where I had lived. The whole time I had worked in the parish of San Miguel, I visited many villages for Mass and prayed for the sick. In the all-night rituals, I stayed throughout the whole ceremony accompanying families as they prayed and consulted the spirits. I ate meals with them without any fanfare that I was the visiting priest. On several occasions, I slept on an adobe bed which seemed to radiate cold. On those occasions, I slept sitting up with minimal exposure to the cold. When we conducted the group meetings, I spent long evenings in various villages in the company of wonderfully friendly people. In none of those visits did I feel a need for greater comfort. Village life suited me well.

Once I made known my intention to marry, most of my colleagues tried to talk me out of marrying. I forgot about my priestly agenda and said simply that I loved Trinidad and wanted to marry her. Jerry McCrane, our regional superior, talked to me about famous people who loved each other with intensity but did not marry because each was already committed to another person. He gave examples of various celebrities whose lives were so exposed to the public while they maintained fidelity to their spouses. Nonetheless, he did recognize I truly loved Trinidad.

Others felt that I was making a mistake. Some talked to me about the wide gap in educational and cultural backgrounds between the two of us. This was probably the strongest and most voiced argument against my marrying. I stated that my plan was to settle in Peru and work with the people as a member of the community. Also, we planned to open a restaurant to support us.

Leaving was not easy. It took me close to two years to decide definitively that I wanted to leave Maryknoll and get married. During that time, I went back to Maryknoll in New York where I went to weekly counseling. I talked frequently with colleagues and eventually announced my decision to leave Maryknoll. The final step toward this decision came when I made a retreat for spiritual reflection and renewal. It was a Jesuit retreat along the rules of St. Ignatius, the founder of the Jesuits. My prayer was that I find some sign or illumination as to what path to follow. As I arrived at the retreat site, I prayed and went to the chapel. There was a Bible in the aisle on a stand about halfway to the altar. I went up to the Bible and opened it. The text that appeared before me was from Jeremiah:

> Thus says the Lord of hosts, the God of Israel, to all the exiles whom I have exiled from Jerusalem to Babylon: Build houses to dwell in; plant gardens, eat their fruits. Take wives and beget sons and daughters; find wives for your sons and give your daughters husbands so that they may bear sons and daughters. There you must increase in number, not decrease. Promote the welfare of the city to which I have exiled you; pray for it to the Lord, for upon its welfare depends your own (Jeremiah 29, 4–7).

Perhaps it was naïve of me to see these words as the sign I was looking for. To many, it may seem too literal an interpretation for me to make such a life-changing decision. Some may say that this is not the way to interpret Scriptures. Yet I have always read the Bible and to me this was the defining touch to help me decide what to do. I was going to marry Trinidad and work for the good of the Aymara community. Ironically, shortly after this retreat, Trinidad sent me a copy of her husband's death certificate. He had returned to Ilave in extremely bad health and died shortly after. Trinidad was free to marry.

My leaving was not turning away from the mission I had started but as a continuum. I was putting into practice what I had wanted all along. I left the Catholic priesthood but not my religion. I wanted to be with the people as a Catholic Christian, not as a ritual power for their religion. I believe that this is the way God acts and intervenes in history and we are the ones to point out those movements.

I wanted to show the equality of the Aymara. I married an Aymara woman of limited education but she was the most important person in my life. To me she represented the whole of the Aymara nation. I did not try too hard to find someone who was more educated and more sophisticated and a worldly person. I wanted one of the poor, one of the invisible persons. She was poor but hardly invisible. She knew her mind and let it be known readily. By marrying into this community, I came closer to becoming a spokesman for the Aymara and for autochthonous groups. In spite of my planning, however, there were several things I did not take into account. The first was that when I returned to Ilave, the pastor approached me and told me I had to move from Ilave. The reason he gave was that I made the priests look bad. I complied and moved to Puno. With that move, I lost track of Marcelino. I no longer had a car at my disposal and did not visit Ilave long enough to go find and visit Marcelino. He was later employed by the Maryknoll Sisters to help in their work with the communities.

Shortly after settling in Puno, we opened a coffee shop called Nic Nac, specializing in pizza, burritos, and apple pie because we wanted to attract tourists. I wanted tourists to stay in Puno for two or three days, set up trips to villages where people would meet with Aymara villagers face to face and get to know them as real people and not as tourist attractions. Also, this plan would increase tourism in Puno which would bring income to the local businesses. Ordinarily, tourists arrived in Puno from Cuzco in time to board the evening boat to Bolivia. They hardly gave Puno a glance. I made my plan known to the Ministry of Tourism. We even visited an island that could receive tourists for an overnight stay. So, Puno could become an educational experience for visitors.

The second thing I did not count on was the government. There were already two plainclothes policemen assigned to watch us. They came by the coffee shop periodically to visit but did not buy anything. One time we were summoned to the office of the PIP because we were using hand-made receipts in our shop. The two policemen who kept track of us delivered the summons and coached us on how to respond, including a gift of typing paper to the interrogating officer. Two months later, one evening after Trinidad had gone home from running the coffee shop, I stayed to serve people after the second showing of local movies. Our coffee shop was right next to the movie theater. The consul who had renewed my visa several times saw me working at the coffee shop. He told me to see him at his office the next day.

When I showed up, he had a book of laws already open to show me my violation; he told me that this was a law, though not promulgated publicly but was very much a law. He showed me a list of nationalities not permitted in Peru. United States citizens were on top of the list, along with Africans, Cubans and Chileans among others. The consul stated that the law also stipulated that no foreigner could hold an administrative position in Peru. Since our shop was a small business, I was accused of being in an administrative position and had to leave the country. In that instant, my dreams and goals were destroyed and I was in shock. I accepted the consul's word and asked how much time I had before leaving. He asked me how much time I needed. I said three months. He agreed and let me go back to my daily routine, but with a new worry.

After leaving the consul's office, I told Trinidad about having to leave. I said, "You have to go, too. I can't just leave you." She agreed readily. I thought she would object to leaving her native country, but it turned out that she had always dreamed of going to the U.S. She had often told me that when she was little and shepherded sheep, she had played building bridges. When other children asked what she was doing, she would tell them, "These are the bridges of San Francisco." I do not know and, neither does she know, how she got this idea about San Francisco. Maryknoll or other American missionaries had not yet come to the area. She would even tell her playmates that one day she was going to San Francisco. Now her dream was coming true as we were obliged to leave Peru.

The fact that Trinidad was now going with me to the United States made me reflect on the many changes that took place for all. The Aymara participants in refection groups had discovered themselves with a new direction in their lives; Maryknoll missionaries had initiated a new way to relate to their parishioners once they saw their ancient religiosity; and I had changed as well as Trinidad. In all these phases of change, each group created a participated change, an evolution under their control. They were not pushed by change but created the new mode of living.

Epilogue

Where I Am Now

I BEGAN THIS BOOK as a man consecrated to religion and spirituality, a gung-ho missionary with a full commitment to know the Aymara people. I grew to love them deeply and wanted to settle among them and dedicate my life to them. Then, I loved a woman and all changed. I married her and tried to obtain a residency visa in Peru but was denied because I was a member of one of the various nationalities then denied residency. I was obliged to return to the United States with my Aymara wife.

My parents were not too happy with my new lifestyle. Years back when I told them I wanted to be a priest; they were totally opposed to the idea. My father had strong anticlerical ideas and words, but slowly he changed. Both he and my mom became heavily involved in many parish activities. My no longer being a priest did not lessen their contributions to their parish. Somehow, they felt as if they had lost face with my new status. In the mid-forties, we had moved from Texas to Anaheim, California, only to face anti-Mexican prejudices until I went off to the seminary. Our social status changed drastically to a more favorable acceptance. My parents felt that their social status was about to change, but it did not. My two brothers and my sister could not understand why I left and married an Aymara woman. Slowly they became more used to seeing me with my Native-American wife, especially once we had two children, Walter and Elizabeth.

After settling in the United States, the one experience I wanted to carry with me was that of healing. While in Peru, Marcelino's spirituality and restorative ability had moved me to the point that I had wanted to heal others. I often felt that Marcelino was training me to provide spiritual healing. This desire to heal had come true when two Sisters, one a Franciscan and the other, a Sister of Mercy, were visiting the Dominican Sisters at San Miguel, our parish. While I was visiting them and carrying on a light conversation with them, one sister asked me if I had been baptized in the Spirit. When I said no, they asked if I wanted to be so baptized. I said yes and they laid hands on my head and started praying. What happened to me was something I had never experienced. I saw myself at a shoreline with huge waves coming over me. Everything was dark except for the waves and me. The waves pounded at me, soaked me and filled me. I did not drown nor did I need air. This was the Holy Spirit taking hold of me. Now I was convinced to heal.

When I visited sick parishioners in Ilave, I would take two Sisters with me and we placed our hands over the head of the sick person and prayed for healing. We witnessed three real healings in the process. One was of a woman who was weak and listless in bed and could hardly talk. She was at Mass the following Sunday, completely well and very grateful to us for prayers. Another was also a woman whose family described her as dying; she also became well after our praying over her. The third person was a woman who suffered from frequent hemorrhaging. She claimed that our touch had cured her and did not bleed any more after our prayers. We always prayed in threes so that the healing was not attributed to one person but to the action of the Holy Spirit. These incidents in Peru had convinced me to become involved in curing, mending and restoring.

These healings began from my having discovered the spirituality of the Aymara. Actually, this recognition was not one of finding something new and previously unknown, since we all have and express the spiritual side of our being. We have the task of discovering the spirituality of people we meet in our lives. Spirituality is not religion but the spiritual presence that rises from one's religion. For Catholics, it is identified in the Mass and in prayer, lots of prayers. For the Buddhist, it is in the chanting; for the Muslim, the Qur'an, especially when sung to best remember the Surahs and verses of the Qur'an. The five pillars of the Sikhs[1] awaken spirituality, which in turn inspires us to recognize the Spirit.

My having studied theology, as well as teaching world religions classes in Arizona, helped me recognize this truth, that we all express a spirituality

1 Kesh (uncut hair, Kangha (wooden comb for hair), Kara (iron bracelet), Kachera (cotton underwear), (Kirpan) sword. *Sikh Religions* pp. 318- 319.

and that we can open ourselves to the presence of the Spirit. We do not need to convert to a religion different from the one we hold. As we discover the spirituality of the other, we begin to eliminate criticizing the religion of the other and avoid competing to bring members into our religious family. We respect each other and are open to the Spirit as found in each relation or meeting between peoples.

However, the various occupations I held were not in a religious environment, and healing through the Spirit was not appropriate. But, healing through stories came to me when I was a case worker from 1978 to 1984 for Hispanic families with developmentally disabled children. These families, who lived throughout Orange County, California, tended to treat their children as sick. I tried to have them understand that their children were normal to a degree and should be raised as normal to their level of growth. I explained to the agency's psychologist, Dr. Jay Robinson, about what I was trying to accomplish with these families. He suggested that I read *Frogs into Princes*, a book about neuro-linguistic programming (NLP), a therapeutic method of changing behavior or attitudes almost instantaneously. Change happens because people know what they have to do but are deterred by behaviors or mindsets that come from low self-esteem, anxiety or simply conforming to a way of non-productive thinking or acting. I am not an NLP therapist, but I know that a story, proverb or a simple word can direct a person to think and act differently. The saying "A word to the wise is sufficient" moves many to correct possibly bad behavior. I had begun implementing this NLP approach but was not successful with these families because I changed jobs and then worked as an employment counselor.

I moved to Arizona in 1987 where I continued as a job search counselor with various agencies since each depended on available government funding. My work life varied from case worker, job counselor and job search specialist for homeless heads of families. I also taught at Western International University in Phoenix and at Chandler-Gilbert Community College over a period of twenty-three years. Currently I volunteer at a St. Vincent de Paul pantry and have served as president of that conference.

In all of these occupations, I brought in healing talks, lessons and life orientation that I had learned from *Frogs into Princes* and some NLP workshops in Arizona. The result was my participation in a number of astonishing changes in individuals' behavior. One example was that of a young man who kept coming to the job counseling center, dressed in loose jeans, a weather-beaten jacket, and wearing a variety of metal jewelry on his person and on his clothes. He wore his hair long and leaned his head, covering his face when I talked to him. After several conversations, I asked him what he wanted since he did not seem to respond to our program. He wanted to be a pilot, a training we did not fund. I told him he could work at the airport where he would meet with pilots to find out how he could study and train. He stood up as if ready to go to the airport. I told him that he had to dress up for an interview, get a haircut, and dress with a clean shirt and tie. I asked him, "How surprised would you be to change?" He said he would be very surprised. He showed up the next day well groomed, in white shirt, tie and slacks. He was on his way to a new life. This was the closest I got to healing in the Spirit.

Just as I began a life consecrated to religion and spirituality, I find it impossible to move away from seeing the action of the Spirit in others. This creates for me a deep love for others, especially people in need. Dialogue with them awakens their spiritual wisdom to begin to resolve issues that confront them. This kind of dialogue with people in need encourages their spiritual resources that heal, restore and begin a new real life.

Even with my having left the official ministry in the Church, I continued to rely on the Spirit to guide me in the healing of others. I still look to the Scriptures to seek the healing stories or parables and the metaphors Jesus used to turn people's attention from their impoverished or sinful state to a clean and spiritually healthy life. As in the Scriptures, I have identified many stories and words that correspond to people's lives. Finding them and implementing them is what I share as a way to bring people to understand and accept each other, a gift I have received from the Holy Spirit, and from Marcelino and I pass it on to my readers.

Glossary

Achachila, (plu.) achachilanaca: grandfather; name applied to the hill spirits

Ajayu: the life-giving soul, anima

Anawim: the poor of God

Anchanchu: a vampire-like spirit that visits sleeping victims to extract blood or fat from the victim.

apóstol misa: 12 rows of coca leaf triads, representing the 12 principal achachilanaca or apostles

ch'iuchi misa: small figures made of metal used in offerings to mother earth and the hill spirits

chuño: freeze dry potatoes

Ch'utas: small fires ignited on Pentecost Sunday; they produce a low-lying smoke over the fields as a sign of gratitude to the fields

Chhijjchi: hail

Compadre: (literally) co-parent; a strong bond between parent and co-parent involving care of the children and providing mutual support between adults.

Conscientização, concientización: the perception of social, political and economic contradictions and to take action against the oppressive elements of reality; social commitment

cuti misa: offering to the spirits to undo a curse or to take revenge on those causing injuries or injustice

dulce misa: an offering to mother earth and to the spirits; ritual elements made of candy ex opere operato: theological concept that sacraments produce grace of themselves, apart and distinct from the language, or even the moral disposition of the person conferring the sacrament.

Gentile: literally, heathen; term applied to the *huaca*, the place of a former idol; applied to ancient burial sites

Huaca: an ancient burial ground, a site to worship ancient spirits

Illapa: ancient name for lightning; Illapa Santiago: St. James, the hurler of lightning bolts

Imilla, pl. imillanaca: little girls, also the name given to 3 potatoes (Janc'o, wila and ch'iara: white, red and black potatoes)

jakejj jalanta: the time of scarcity for people

Juyphi: frost

Llima: grasses that grow in a river

Liq'ich'iri, also known as kharisiri: usually a Franciscan, or any priest, who wanders about at night to hypnotize his victims and then collect human fat for making the holy oils used in church rituals.

Mullu: stone figure or talisman of various focuses and said to be the residing place of the spirit of that subject depicted in the mullu.

Pacco: sorcerer, magician

Pachamama: Mother earth, spirit of fertility and life

Paksi: lady moon, mamita paksi

Q'intu: three leaves of coca used to invoke a spirit.

Qamasa: the shadow soul

Supaya: devil, evil spirit

Thaya: wind spirits

Tutuka: dust devil; small whirlwind that kicks up dust and small debris; related to thaya

Uyhuiri: the guardian spirit of a household

Uywa jalanta: period of scarcity for animals

Viracocha: Also, Wiracoha or Huirajocha: Son of Inti, the sun god; Huirajocha applied to non-Indian men now seen as masters.

Yatiri: seer, healer, diviner

Bibliography

Published Sources

Allen, Roland. *Missionary Methods St Paul's or Ours?* Grand Rapids, Michigan: Wm. B. Eerdmans Publishing Co. 1962.

Arriaga, Pablo Joseph. *The Extirpation of Idolatry in Peru.* Trans. L. Clark Keating. Lexington: University of Kentucky, 1968.

Bertonio, P. Ludovico. *Vocabulario de la Lengua Aymara.* Edición facsimilaria. Leipzig, B.G. Teubner, 1847.

Bosch, David J. *Transforming Mission: Paradigm Shifts in Theology of Mission.* New York: Orbis,, 1991.

Buber, Martin. *Eclipse of God.* Amherst, New York: Humanity Books, 1952.

———. *I and Thou.* Trans. Ronald Gregor Smith. New York: Collier Books, 1958.

Cieza de León, Pedro. *The Discovery and Conquest of Peru.* Ed. and trans. Alexandra Parma Cook and David Noble Cook. Durham: Duke University Press, 1998.

Cobo, Bernabe. *History of the Inca Empire.* Trans. and ed. Roland Hamilton. Austin: University of Texas, 1979.

Cohen, Tom, director. "The Healer." New York: Amram Nowak Associates, 1973.

Farmer, Paul. *Pathologies of Power.* Berkeley, California: University of California Press, 2003.

Fitzpatrick-Behrens, Susan. *The Maryknoll Catholic Mission in Peru.* Notre Dame, Indiana: University of Notre Dame Press, 2011.

Freire, Paulo. *Pedagogy of the Oppressed.* New York: The Continuum Publishing Company, 1970.

Funke, Phyllis. "How One Priest Does His Preaching," *New York Times Archives,* https://timesmachine.nytimes.com/timesmachine/1973/01/28/103217214.html?pagenumber=125.

Gutierrez, Gustavo. *A Theology of Liberation.* Maryknoll, New York: Orbis, 1988.

Harris, Thomas A. *I'm OK- You're OK.* New York: Harper and Rowe, 1973.

Huaman Poma de Ayala, Felipe. *Letter to a King.* Ed. and trans. Christopher Dilke. New York: E.P Dutton, 1978.

Jung, Carl G. *Memories, Dreams and Reflections.* Ed. Aniela Jaffe. Trans. Richard and Clara Winston. New York: Vintage Books, 1989.

———. *Man and His Symbols.* New York: Dell, 1968.

Kolata, Alan. *Valley of the Spirits.* New York: John Wiley and Sons, 1996.

Merklinger, Philip, "Spiritual Ecology: A Preliminary Sketch." *Philosophy and Theology*, vol. 20 (2008).

Ortega Perrier, Marietta. "Andean Metaphysical Concepts and the Role of Imagery in Catholic Religious Instruction," *Diálogo Andino*, no. 50 (January 6, 2016): 167–180.

Pope John Paul II, *Catechism of the Catholic Church*. Vatican City: Liberia Editrice Vaticana, 1994.

Pope Paul VI. "Sacrosanctum Concilium." *Constitution on the Sacred Liturgy*, November 18, 1965," no. 48: <http://www.scborromeo.org>.

———. Second Vatican Council, *"Nostra Aetate: Constitution on the Sacred Liturgy,"* Rome, 1965. Ed. Walter M. Abbott. New York: Guild, 1966.

Sikh Missionary Center, *Sikh Religions*. Ann Arbor, Michigan: Sheridan Books, Inc., 1990.

St. Augustine, *The Confessions of St. Augustine*. Trans. E.B. Pusey. New York: Barnes and Noble, 1999.

Stahl, Fernando. *En el País de los Incas*. Buenos Aires: Casa Editorial Sudamericana Florida F.C.C.C.A., 1935.

Tschopik, Harry. *The Aymara of Chucuito, Peru*. New York: American Museum of Natural History, 1955.

Turner, Victor. *The Ritual Process*. New York, Cornell University Press, 1969.

Unamuno, Miguel. *San Manuel Mártir*. Madrid: Colección Letras Hispanas, Edición Cátedra, 1991.

Vega, Garcilaso de la. *El Inca, Royal Comentaries of the Incas and General History of Perú*. vol. 1. Trans. Harold V. Livermore. Austin: University of Texas Press, 1966.

www.ingramcontent.com/pod-product-compliance
Lightning Source LLC
Chambersburg PA
CBHW060401090426
42734CB00011B/2221